THE PROFESSIONAL BONDSMAN

How to Start and Operate Your Own Bail Bond Agency

BY RICHARD WILLS

SECOND EDITION

DRAGON PRESS

First Printing June 1996

Library of Congress Number 94-72703
ISBN 0-9622822-7-8

Second Edition
Published by: THE DRAGON PRESS

Cover design by: Richard Wills and Ken Wong

Printed in the United States of America

10 9 8 7 6 5 4 3 2

Dear Friend,

Just the other day I read in an opinion poll that stated
"crime is the was the #1 concern in today's society".
It is a subject matter that many of us care not to discuss openly, because
it's frightening as well as a cancer that angers us and robs our
communities of their cohesiveness.
For all of the bad that crime does in society, few of us take advantage of
the situation.

The Professional Bondsman should be viewed with care.
Crime in America is now a business... big business.
Organized criminals, cartels and gangs are busy committing crimes at
alarming rates. Private enterprises are now being used to patrol our
streets and neighborhoods providing protection that the public police are
unable to furnish.

There are more prisons being built than universities and colleges. Many
correctional functions such as prisoner transportation and guards are
being provided by the private sector instead of state or federal agencies.
An estimated 14,648,700 arrests were made in the U.S. in 1995.

All of this should tell you something... Crime Pays!
(If you're in the right business).

You don't need any special training or a degree to become a
Bail Bondsman.
Many secrets of this lucrative business that you will be exposed to will
stay with you forever. Whether you decide to become a bail bondsman or
not, you'll know what to do if a friend or loved one winds up in jail.

Consider this book as an investment.

Many happy investments returns,

Richard Wills

ACKNOWLEDGEMENTS

This volume exists not because of crime in America, but because of the opportunities available in this business enterprise. Crime is an epidemic that affects us all, one way or another. And as long as teenagers are steadily growing up to become adults, crime will be something society has to deal with.

Many thanks go out to the Professional Bondsmen who helped to make this book possible. Without their years of knowledge and experience in the business, this book would not exist.

The purpose of this book is to provide the reader with a realistic as possible picture regarding the opportunities available in the bail bond business. It is designed as a roadmap to success for aspiring bail bondsmen/women.

The book focuses on starting your business, staying in business, negotiating and when to write a bond. In addition to the experted focus on daily operations of the business, actual cases are described and discussed.

Preparing for the Bail Agent's exam and possible questions are featured... you will also find forms and documents used in the business necessary for the novice or veteran to operate as a professional in the business, plus much more. It is written unbiased to give an accurate as possible view of this lucrative business.

CONTENTS

FOREWORD

This manual was written due to the hundreds of clients, friends and relatives who have asked me — "How Do You Get Into The Bail Bond Business?" At the time when people were asking me about getting into this business, I told them what 10 to 20 other bondsmen told me when I tried to get started — "It's hard and it's rough... it's not an easy business to get into". Followed by the most discouraging factor — "You'll need at least $50,000 cash along with some real estate to put up as collateral with an insurance company".

After hearing this speech 10 to 20 times anyone would be discouraged from venturing into the bail bond business. But you know what, this was only a smoke screen to deter me and countless others from getting into a multi-million dollar business.

My curiosity about this business led me to many universities, libraries and bookstores in an attempt to find out how one would go into this type of business. To my amazement, there was absolutely no information on the subject. I couldn't believe it.

My determination to work in this industry led me to a bondsman who needed help, and he let me work for him (with no pay). That's right, I worked for free just to get my foot in the door of this fascinating business. I learned the old fashioned way — I earned it. After I was trained in the business and knew what I was doing, I hardly ever saw my boss. He would be out golfing, fishing, and traveling while I did all of the work.

You now have in your hands the New 2nd Edition, completely updated, which features subject matter previously known exclusively to longtime veteran bondsmen already working in the business. This new edition tells you about the different types of bonds you will come in contact with, such as federal bonds, appeal bonds and even writing a bond for traffic warrants. There is a special topic covering filing motions and how to check docket sheets which will keep you in business.

Throughout the book, actual case studies are examined, showing you exactly what could happen in the course of bailing someone out of jail up until the time when the case is finished. These case studies will give you a valuable lesson in the art of becoming a professional bondsman, whether you are just beginning, or an old pro in the business.

The most requested subject in this new second edition is the Bail Agent's Exam. This section gives you an idea of what to expect when applying for a bail agent's license. Although the requirements may vary from state to state, there is much to be gained in this segment.

You will encounter possible questions to expect when taking the exam, along with excerpts from the California Administrative Code governing bail bonds. Also featured, is a section entitled "Tips for Success", taken from the files of a professional bondsman who've been there.

While developing this second edition I had one critical decision, whether it should be a formal, fully documented legal guide, or instead a book of more general interest that can be applied in the real world. I chose the latter because the actual operations and functions of this business have never been written down or published. You have to learn as you go. That is the only way to learn this business.

My hope is that the book will be serious and complete enough to be useful to laymen as well as veteran bondsmen, lawyers and other professionals interested in this little-known business.

This book tells in detail, what it takes to start and operate your own bail bond agency. By using this manual as your vehicle to get started in this lucrative industry you can start raking in the financial rewards that this business has to offer.

INTRODUCTION: ORIGIN OF THE U.S. BAIL SYSTEM

What does the word "bail" bring to mind? First of all it has a variety of legal implications. They all deal with the situation whereas one holds something or someone of value for another. By tracing the word bail from it's earliest origin, some scholars say that the word is derived from the old French word bailee, meaning to deliver, or a container used to remove water from a boat.

Sir Edward Cooke, former Lord Chief Justice of the King's Bench, in his Treatise of Bail and Mainprize, states that "baily is an old Saxon word, and signifieth a safekeeper or protector... and therefore when a man upon surety is delivered out of prison... he is delivered into bayle-that is, into their safekeeping or protection from prison".

Some scholars even suggest that modern bail comes from the laws of old English governing debt, from the ancient concept of wergeld. Governed by this ancient stratagem, a person who was accused of committing a wrong had to guarantee a payment to reimburse that wrong, should he later be found at fault.

Just as modern day surety guarantees, at the risk of his/her own personal loss, the presence of the accused at trial under the modern bail system, so in primal English society did surety assure that a debtor would pay his wergeld to compensate the victim of a wrong.

Victims of injury were assured of some redress under this program without having to fight it out, thus resulting to personal vendettas. To avoid all of this, a neutral party would come between the creditor and debtor, like a mediator or trustee. By guaranteeing performance he would escape bodily harm of the accused or other resorts to reprisal.

The promise of the surety guaranteed the victim (creditor) that the debtor would be in attendance and would pay his wergeld if debtor were to be found at fault. If the guilty party did not pay his/her obligated debt, the surety ended up assuming that responsibility. This type of agreement was a contractual correlation like bail.

The modern system of bail today is intended as a device to make sure that a person charged with a crime will be available for trial. As you can see, the evolution of the bail system is quite visible. Although certain procedures have changed, the concept still remains the same.

CHAPTER 1: THE BAIL BOND BUSINESS

So you want to be a Bail Bondsman... then consider the following: Some type of crime is committed every two seconds in the U. S. This includes misdemeanors as well as felonies.

Murder, rape, robbery, assault, burglary, larceny-theft, motor vehicle theft, vandalism, embezzlement, arson, fraud, forgery and counterfeiting, vagrancy, gambling, drug abuse violations, sex offenses, prostitution, weapons violations, curfew and loitering law violations, shoplifting, receiving, possessing or buying stolen property, offenses against family and children, mayhem, drunkness and driving under the influence are just a few of the many offenses that people are arrested on every year and need a bail bondsman to secure their freedom.

The bail bond business is one of the few businesses that seem to thrive in good times as well as in so-called bad times. As long as teenagers are growing up to become adults, crime will continue to plague society.

To operate as a professional bail bondsman means to separate yourself from your business. No one wants to be thought of as someone who puts thieves, con artists and swindlers back on the street to commit more crimes.

The bail bond business is a business just like the banking business. A banker approves loans for applicants who show good, squeaky clean credit history, provide strong collateral and are not too risky for the bank. By the same token a bail bondsman provides bail for clients who provide good strong collateral, has family ties or ties to the community, not a flight risk and are unlikely to put the bonding agency in any type of financial jeopardy.

A major difference between the job functions of the banker and that of the bail bondsman, is that the banker is only in power from 9-5, Monday thru Friday approving loans. While the bail bondsman is in power 24 hours a day, 365 days a year posting bonds and getting people out of jail. When you consider the fact that time is money, then crime pays, if you're in the Bail Bond Business.

GETTING STARTED

The first thing you need to do is ask yourself "Do I really want to become a bail bondsman?" If you answered yes, keep reading. (If you answered "no", still keep reading). Let me be the first to tell you that the bail bond business is not for everyone... but keep in mind as you read this book that everyone can learn something about the ins and outs of this lucrative and secretive business as well as have fun along the way.

You don't need a college degree or any special training to become a bail bondsman. One skill that is desirous is "people handling skills". Since you will be dealing with people, and I mean all types...you should at least enjoy being around them and have a sincere motive to help them achieve their goal of being released from jail.

In this business, the way you start out with a client is the way you end up. The information in this book will more than get you started on the right track to become a successful bail bondsman.

YOUR JOB

The job as a bail bondsman is a simple one — you will specialize in getting people out of jail. When a person is arrested and charged with a criminal offense, this person will need the help of a bail bondsman in order to gain his/her freedom.

When is this need for a bondsman's help set in motion? A man is driving home from work one night. He stops off at a local bar and downs a few drinks. Two blocks from his home, the police stop him. He's belligerent. He fails the sobriety test and gets into a fight with the police. (Should I say more?)

A newlywed couple are having an argument. Some name calling, pushing, shoving and a few broken dishes heat things up. The wife calls the police in order to quell the situation. Police respond. Wife tells police husband is on drugs. Police fail to find drugs in the house, but discover that the wife has several outstanding traffic warrants for her arrest. (Ok, you get the picture, right?)

Normally, when a person is arrested for a crime, he/she goes to jail. Then a bail is set. (Crimes in which the arrestee may face the death penalty are not bailable, i.e., murder.)

After a bail is set, the arrestee is eligible for release from jail. By contacting the jail where the arrestee is detained, you (the bondsman), will find out the bail amount set, the charges and other pertinent information that will enable you to negotiate with the indemnitor (person putting up money and/or collateral) for the arrestee's release. Using this information, you can post the bond which will gain the arrestee's freedom. Once you have accomplished getting your client their freedom and putting their feet on the ground, you have earned your fee.

As a professional bail bondsman your obligation is to the court, to see that the defendant makes all court appearances once released. Your job is not necessarily finished once you write the bond and the defendant is released. This is only the beginning. You must follow through on a case until the bond that was written has been exonerated and the case is over. This will be discussed further as we proceed.

INITIAL CONTACTS

The first person(s) to contact in the bail bond business would be to start by contacting some of the bondsmen in your area. Drive by their office and see how they are set up. This will enable you to pick up some valuable tips on how they operate their business.

You could also see if they need any help in their office. This is how I got started, and you can get some good on the job training by doing so. Although, with the information contained in this manual you will learn most of the techniques and secrets that will put you ahead of some of the veterans in the business.

THE DEPARTMENT OF INSURANCE

Every state has an agency or department where you will apply for a bail agents license. This agency or department is usually The Department of Insurance. They will be more than happy to send you the needed material necessary to get started for licensing.

You will want to request an application and any other material needed to apply for a bail bondsman/bail agent's license. In some states, The Department of Insurance may supply you with a booklet to study in order to prepare for the exam.

The exam is nothing to get the jitters about. It's not like taking the Bar Exam or anything like that. It is a simple test, and I have never heard on anyone failing it if they prepared themselves. So do no get nervous. (See Section on Bail Agents Exam and Appendix II for Department of Insurance Commissioners)

SURETY INSURANCE COMPANIES

The only companies authorized to write bail bonds in the United States are called "surety insurance companies". These companies are insurance companies licensed by the State Department of Insurance.

This is where the business function of writing bail bonds begin, at the top. The insurance companies require indemnity from the insurance agents. The insurance agents consequently, require indemnity from the bail bondsman, who ultimately require indemnity from their clients. This straight line business arrangement leaves little risk involved for the parties involved, because collateral is required at every stage of the game.

When contacting one of these surety insurance companies, you will be referred to a managing general agent or a field manager who will be your main contact regarding the requirements for getting a contract in order for you to write bail bonds. They will also assist you with your inventory as well as auditing your books.

All insurance companies have different requirements for qualifying new agents. Be prepared to show a financial statement, and credit check if necessary, to show your stability and net worth. (See Appendix IV for Surety Insurance Companies)

It's a good idea to contact several surety insurance companies so you can compare the different requirements. Also, some of the big surety insurance may have a quota for the number of agents desired in a particular area or region.

Depending on the area and population, a surety insurance company may want only four or five bail agents working a particular region in order to avoid too much competition or saturation. If one surety insurance company turns you down try another one. Also, once you get started you will want to have at least one surety insurance company as a backup.

Special Note: When contacting surety insurance companies whom you wish to write bail bonds for, make sure that they are reputable and recognized in the business. Many of the old-time, veteran jailers will question or will not accept bail bonds from companies that they are not familiar with. In addition to the surety insurance companies listed in the appendix, your local business yellow pages will also prove helpful.

SPECIAL REQUIREMENTS

Some states, such as California require all prospective bail agents to attend a 2-day, 12 hour Pre-licensing Educational Course for Bail Bonds before they are permitted to take the bail bonds exam. The course is given by the California Bail Agents Association located in Sacramento, California. (See Appendix)

All candidates attending the two-day course receive a certificate of completion. This certificate must be presented upon taking the written exam for bail bond licensing.

The course is nothing to get nervous about. It is more or less an introduction to the bail bond exam. This way a candidate will have some basic insights as what to expect on the actual exam. To make it convenient for prospective bail agents, the course is held in different regions throughout the state at various periods.

THE OFFICE

Where you decide to operate your business as a bondsman will be designated as your office. Whether you decide to work as an agent for an established bonding company or open up your own agency, your office must reflect professionalism.

Your image as a professional bondsman will earn you the respect and trust from clients that's needed to make it in this business. When they step into your office they want to be assured that you can solve their problems.

WORKING AT HOME

The bail bond business can be considered a home-based business, depending on your locale. Working from home as your office base is ideal for agents just starting in this business. By using your home as your office, all you really need is an area where you can keep track of everything that your are doing.

Your bedroom, kitchen, den or some place in your home where you can have a small desk or table to work from will suffice. A good night light will be needed because when you are just starting out in this business, your night calls will help you to build your business. Why? Because most of the veteran bondsmen will be sleep and have an answering service or a paging service take their calls after certain hours. This is where you can capitalize, because no one wants to talk to an answering service or leave a message on a voice mail machine...let alone page someone and wait for a returned phone call, when they can easily call another bondsman who can solve their problem and get their friend or loved one out of jail.

Working out of your home will be cost effective because the most that you will need is a telephone, a work area with a table and chair, a calculator and a file box to keep records of bonds written and expenses incurred in the operation of your business.

This type of arrangement is ideal because: (1) You can meet clients at the jail. They will love this especially if they live near the jail where the arrestee is being detained. (2) You can arrange to make house calls, picking up collateral and having indemnitors sign papers in the comfort of their home. You can also make some extra money by charging your clients a posting fee for this service. The community where you will be conducting your business and the hours that you will be transacting business will determine if this is feasible.

AN OFFICE AWAY FROM HOME

A small office suite or even sharing office space with a professional business that compliments the bail bond business is the perfect set up, because eventually you will need some place where your clients can come and visit you. This adds you your professional image.

You've heard the phrase — "Location, location, location" when looking for a new home or business site. Well choosing a site to start your bail bond agency is no exception. Location is one of the most important factors to decide on when starting in this business, just as in any other business.

The very best location for any bail bondsman is directly across the street or next door to a jail facility or police booking station. Why? Because you can generate a tremendous amount of walk-in traffic. These walk-in customers just want to get their party out of jail and they do not care who gets the business.

Most of the times a walk-in customer may already have a regular bondsman that they have been doing business with, but since you happen to be located where their party is in custody, they will prefer doing business with you. Walk-in traffic can mean up to 50% more business for an agency.

Do not be afraid to open up your office where bondsmen are already established because: (1) You can attract some of the regular customers of these bondsmen if you happen to be open when they are closed. (2) Very often, people have a notion to try a new or different bondsman due to poor service or disagreements with their regular bondsman. This will bring new clients. In this business you must take advantage of all opportunities that come your way.

Although choosing a site near a jail facility may be the best location, this does not guarantee an increase in business. Why? Because if your service is poor and you are not able to meet the needs of your customers, you lose.

There are bondsmen located directly across the street from jail facilities, and would you believe, not only is the walk-in traffic poor, the phone rarely rings? The reason for this is because these bondsmen evidently are providing poor services to their clients and are seldom available when needed.

On the other hand, there are bondsmen who are located miles from a jail facility and are doing excellent business. The secret here is that they are centrally located in the community. These bondsmen are able to serve clients over a ten to twenty mile radius. Their success comes from giving good personalized service to clients.

Whether you are located near a jail or even miles from a jail, if you advertise and give good professional service you will generate good business, and your phone will ring. And if the phone rings you have a good chance of writing some bonds and getting paid.

PARKING AND SECURITY

Whether you have on-the-street parking or a huge parking lot for your clients, parking should be safe as well as convenient. You can bet if a client visits your office and returns to his/her car with a parking ticket or a stereo missing, you won't see them again.

Make sure that your office surroundings are well lit at night. A well lighted bail bonds office is not only good for security reasons, but it is excellent advertisement for your business. No one wants to visit a bondsman late at night carrying large sums of cash if the area is poorly lit.

Security should be the top priority for you, your employees and clients. It is best to have some type of alarm system when you are in the office as well as when you are away from the office. Why? Because you will be handling large sums of cash as well as client's collateral. You will also have important documents and records on file at your office. Your files should be fireproof should a fire occur. It's best to be safe than sorry.

Check around in your area for a burglar alarm company that specializes in silent alarm systems. A good system is one that can alert the Police Department in the event of a robbery or break-in. This is not to suggest that you go out and purchase an elaborate alarm system to guard Fort Knox, but you should consider some type of protection, because you never know.

Once you decide on your business locality, you will know what type of security to invest in. By all means have some type of security, even if it's just a hungry watch dog.

OFFICE EQUIPMENT AND SUPPLIES

Should you decide to start out transacting business in an office suite or at home, you should be equipped proficiently. Listed are some of the basic essentials that you will need in order to operate professionally. Some of the items listed are optional.

You decide which ones you can do without until business starts rolling. By no means should you go out and furnish an elaborate office. This list is to give you an idea of what will be needed as you progress in the business.

1. Two Telephone Lines — One line to receive incoming calls from clients and others, and one line to make outgoing calls to jails, indemnitors, courts, etc. Make it a point to get a phone that has a "speaker" function. You will need this because when contacting the jails for bail information you may be put "on hold" for long periods of time. With the speaker function, you can be doing other tasks while waiting.

2. Typewriter/Word Processor — You will want to be distinguished as a professional by having typed reports, etc.

3. Computer — This will allow you to keep track of previous defendants and indemnitors without having them fill out new paperwork when visiting your office. You will probably be able to find software to meet the needs of your business.

4. Copy Machine — This will come in handy to reproduce documents for clients, as well as for yourself.

5. Microfiche Machine — To verify the legitimacy of property to be used as collateral. Also to verify the rightful owner(s) of property being used as collateral.

6. Desk and Chair — For your professional image. Make sure your have enough chairs for your clients.

7. File Cabinet(s) — To keep records, documents, applications and files of every person you have bailed out of jail.

8. Safe or Vault — To store valuable collateral.

9. Two Index Card File Boxes — If you don't have a computer, this will come in handy to keep records of all defendants that you bail out of jail. You can have one file box for open cases and another one for cases still pending.

10. In and Out Basket — To keep track of important correspondence, court appointments and bail forfeitures to be investigated.

11. Celluiar/Mobile Phone or Pager — If something important arises when you are out in the field, you can be contacted immediately.

12. Credit Card Setup — To accept Visa, MasterCard and American Express as form of payment for premium and collateral.

13. Post Authorization — This enables you to accept personal checks without the fear of receiving a "Non Sufficient Fund Notice" from the bank.

14. Penal Code Book — This is a good reference book to educate you regarding codes used in booking prisoners.

15. Optional:

- Small Ice Box	- TV
- Hot Plate or Stove	- Radio
- Water Cooler	- Sofa Bed

EMPLOYEES

Since you will advertise your business as a 24 hour service, you will need some help because you do not want to "burn" yourself out. If you are married, your spouse could prove to be your best backup. The both of you could easily work out a schedule so someone could be available to handle incoming calls and customers at various shifts.

If your spouse is not a good candidate, maybe one of your children or a trustworthy relative, who is of age can do the job. Experience has shown that when just starting out, it's best to have a family member or someone you can really trust to work with you. Why? Because you will be handling large sums of cash and expensive merchandise. These kind of things you don't want to come up missing.

Also an unfaithful or deceitful employee can easily be bribed or persuaded into bailing someone out without the proper collateral via sex, drugs, money you name it. Many bail bond agencies have gone out of business or reduced to near extinct due to weak or resentful employees.

Your next best employee is a good answering service or beeper service that can accept your calls and contact you when a bond call comes in. Most bondsmen that I know use this type of setup rather than hire a secretary to answer for them.

The only drawback from using an answering service or other recording or paging device is that when a bond call comes in, the person who is calling wants immediate action. And if they have to talk to a machine or someone other than the bondsman, they are likely to call another bondsman and give him the business. But once you are established and have a reputation with regular customers, they will want to do business with you and only you. And they won't mind waiting for you to return their phone call.

If you decide to hire outside help, try and get employees who are looking for a future and want to grow with your company. Get them bonded for security purposes and if possible do a background check. A good incentive when hiring a new employee is to get them licensed as a bail agent after they have been with you over a certain period of time, maybe after one year of service.

Give it some deep thought as to who could you trust and depend on before you open your bail bond agency. If no one comes to mind, just do it yourself. As you progress in the business, you will know exactly what type of person(s) that will fit in with your office setup. As mentioned, when just starting out you do not need a lot of unnecessary expenses.

CHAPTER 2: OPERATING YOUR BUSINESS

Operating a bail bond business is a little different from operating a gas station or hamburger stand. The day-to-day operations at a gas station or hamburger stand basically consist of customers placing an order, paying for the goods or service and leaving. You may or may not ever see the same customer again in life

Now take the bail bond business. In order to receive service, a client must first qualify. The bondsman will basically know the life history of a client. Everything is verified...name, address, telephone number, employment history, work telephone number, work address, work supervisor, social security number, income, rent, credit history, friends and relatives as references as well as any other pertinent information.

Just about anybody can operate at a secondary level of a business, but to operate like a pro in the bail bond business, takes the acme of skill and alertness... which you are about to learn.

WHEN CLIENTS CALL

A good policy when dealing with your clients is to treat every client as if he/she was your first client. Treat the new clients as if they were long time customers, and treat the old customers as if they were brand new. Customers like that personal feeling when they do business with you.

They will patronize your business just the same as that of a doctor or lawyer. They will call on you only when they need you.

Believe it or not, when you get certain people out of jail, it's almost compared to saving their life. (I'm not talking about career criminals who make their livelihood out of breaking the law and going to jail, but the hard working citizen who may have been victimized by the system).

The bondsman has a "divine-like" power, so to speak. Think about it...who else has the power to raise a frightened citizen from the depths of jail? The incarcerated person may have been at the wrong place at the wrong time, or did a little too much celebrating and ended up in jail. Whatever the case may be, they will never forget you... the bondsman.

When a customer calls or visits your office, remember this one thing, "Always be in control". By this, I mean that you must control the tone of the conversation without being rude or discourteous. You can bet that if you don't control the conversation, your client surely will. Your job is to get some important answers from a client in order to bail a person out of jail.

Some clients will begin a conversation telling you about how the person got arrested... who was arrested with them... how the police mistreated them... that the person is innocent... that they must get the person out because they may lose their job, etc. This can go on and on unless you take control of the conversation. In order to take control of a bond call, the 11 Master Questions will be your tool. (To Be Discussed Later)

Always keep in mind that when a client calls or visits you, they need help in bailing someone out of jail. They are not visiting your office to "chew the fat". You will be paid by how well you negotiate getting the incarcerated person out of jail and on the streets as soon as possible. When people are spending money with you to bail someone out of jail, they expect you to operate in a professional manner and know what you're doing, this goes a long way.

This is one business where word of mouth can prove to be one of your best means of advertisement. You never know who will call you for a bond, so it is good to treat all clients like gold.

CASE STUDY

A while back, the author did business with a little old church going lady we'll call Miss Daisey. She was referred by a former client. Her problem: Her grandson was in jail. His bail was $17,000.00, and the charge was rape.

When she called, it was four o'clock in the morning and she had no cash on hand. All of her money was in the bank, but she said that her property to be used as collateral was paid for, free and clear. The property checked out to be valid and everything looked good. Miss Daisey had no transportation to come into the bail bond office, but she lived near the jail where her grandson was being detained.

The bondsman, after calling the jail and receiving the bail information, asked Miss Daisey "how she intended to pay the 10% premium," which was $1,700.00? She said that she could write a check for $1,700.00 to cover the premium... she also promised to pick up the check, first thing in the morning as soon as the banks opened and bring in $1,700.00 cash in exchange for the check.

On this verbal agreement, she was met at the jail where she handed over the personal check for $1,700.00 and her grandson was released. Now, she called her regular bondsman as well as five other bondsmen, with no luck. Why? Because she didn't have cash for the 10% premium.

Very, very few bondsmen will take a chance on receiving a personal check when bailing someone out. It's just too risky. If the check should bounce, the bondsman is stuck and the defendant goes his/her merry way.

With the advent of new technology bondsmen are now able to accept personal checks from customers and have funds deposited into their account immediately without the fear of the check bouncing. This is something worth considering when you start your business.

SYNOPSIS

A chance was taken in this transaction because of the way the indemnitor talked, the fact that she was referred by a reliable client and she passed the test of the 11 Master

Questions. Also, her property was verified to be free and clear of any liens. So, if her grandson decided to jump bail, foreclosing on the property would have been the remedy to get paid, if it came to that.

She kept her word, picked up the check and gave the bondsman $1,700.00 cash in exchange for the check. And believe it or not, her grandson's case turned out to be a D.A. reject (meaning that no case was filed for lack of evidence or victim recanted story). This was an easy $1,700.00 made for less that an hour's work. Although cases like this don't come everyday, it just goes to show you that you cannot overlook any of your clients that call.

NEGOTIATING

Negotiating a bond is a art, an acquired skill that only a few in the business have mastered. Just like in any business, there are secrets, short-cuts and strategies that are applied to limit risk involvement... and the bail bond business is no different.

No one can take the entire risk out of writing a bond, but what we have done here is to minimize the risk to such a great degree that the onus will fall on the indemnitor, and not the bonding company.

THE 11 MASTER QUESTIONS

Just how do you qualify a defendant for bail? There is no general rule of thumb on this because each case is different. The bail bond business is not a gas station type operation or a liquor store where a customer pulls up and gets five bucks worth of gas or booze and drives into the sunset — not hardly.

In this business, the more you know about the people that you are dealing with, i.e., a defendant and indemnitor, the easier it is to qualify the defendant for a bond. Knowing how to qualify a defendant for bail is one of the most important ingredients in writing a bond. Once you know the right questions to ask when you are negotiating a bond, you will save precious time and money.

The negotiating procedure described here is considered to be one of the best, if not the best, in qualifying a potential client for bail. Write each one of the Master Questions down on an index card and carry them with you until you have memorized them. (You will ask these questions to the person(s) negotiating bail for the arrestee who is in custody.)

1. WHEN WAS DEFENDANT ARRESTED?

Asking this question first tells you a great deal about the person in jail. If the defendant has been in custody for over a week, the party negotiating for the defendant's bail have probably called every bondsman in town by now, with no luck. (Collateral shaky, possible new charges added to defendant, etc.) As you proceed in your negotiations, keep this in mind. Also, if a person has been in jail over a week, don't be afraid to ask the indemnitor(s) why this person hasn't been released yet. Nine times out of ten, they will give you an honest answer.

The majority of your business will be from defendants who were just arrested or may have been in jail for no longer that one or two days. When this happens, you'll probably be the first bondsman that the indemnitors have contacted, so you want to act fast in qualifying the client.

NOTE: On some occasions, a defendant may have had to stay in jail for a certain period of time in order to see a judge for a bail reduction, traffic warrants, parole violations, etc. These factors may cause a defendant to be in custody for a week or more. As mentioned, always used discretion in all bail negotiating situations, because each bond is different.

2. BAIL AMOUNT

Asking the question "How much is the bail?" will inform you as to the seriousness of the crime and exactly what type of collateral will be necessary to write the bond. The rule of thumb is: The larger the bail amount - the more collateral required.

Always get enough collateral on a bond that you write so that you will be in a position to recover easily, should you have to. In California, most bondsmen prefer property (real estate) as collateral along with the 10% premium in order to write a bond. Although you will see that real estate is not essentially the only collateral to accept.

3. DEFENDANT'S EMPLOYMENT. WHERE? HOW LONG?

Not all people arrested are criminals or bad people. A lot of innocent hard working citizens go to jail everyday due to mistaken identity, being at the wrong place at the wrong time, and so on. A defendant who has been on the job for 5-10 years or longer, and work for a well known company such as A.T.&T., the Federal Government, etc. is a far better risk that a defendant who is unemployed or someone who drifts from job to job.

Your main concern when bailing someone out of jail is that the defendant be present for all court appearances. This is your obligation to the court system as a bail bondsman. A person with a good job and family is not likely to uproot everything and disappear on you. So you see, you have something positive and strong if a potential client has stable employment and strong ties with his family and community.

4. INDEMNITOR'S EMPLOYMENT. WHERE? HOW LONG?

Asking whether the person signing (indemnitor) is employed is a significant question also. This will tell you what type of individual(s) you are dealing with. Nine times out of ten, if the indemnitor has a reputable job and is a responsible person, they will see to it that the defendant makes all court appearances when scheduled. The indemnitor does not want to take chances on forfeiting any collateral nor going through any unnecessary changes associated with a defendant missing court.

5. DOES INDEMNITOR OWN PROPERTY?

As mentioned, in California real property is the main type of collateral accepted to bail out a defendant, although it is not the only type. The thing about accepting real estate as collateral is that you are in excellent position to recover any loss should there be a bail forfeiture... And anytime there is a bail forfeiture, the responsibility falls on the you, the bondsman.

5a. If the signer (indemnitor) is buying property, the signer must have deeds to prove ownership. When you start writing bonds, you will become familiar with the types of deeds to accept. With the use of a microfiche that has a record of all properties recorded in your county, you can immediately locate a property being used as collateral and know if the deed being used is valid or not.

There are various ways of checking out a property to be used as collateral. You may be able to work something out with a title insurance company or some other business establishment in your area for this service. Some of these companies will charge you a monthly fee and give you a verbal over the telephone as to whether a property being used as collateral is good or not.

6. NAME PROPERTY LISTED IN?

This is a very important question in your negotiations because the name(s) that appears on the deed... these same names must sign the bail agreement and trust deeds from your office. The property that is being used as collateral is no good if the deed shows two or three owners, and only one of the owners will sign.

Never accept a deed as collateral that is not properly signed by all of the owners. This will protect you in the long run should you ever have to take legal actions to recover a loss.

7. LOCATION OF PROPERTY

The location of the property to be used collateral is crucial. When you first start out in this business it is best to accept only property in your area that you can check out and verify. Accepting property in another county or state that cannot be verified is very risky.

Also be wary of property located in a poor, run down area of town or vacant land to be used as collateral, especially on a large bond. You may want to inspect the property first and/or require additional collateral from the indemnitor.

8. DATE PROPERTY PURCHASED?

A signer who has been in their property five (5) years or more is a good risk, considering any liens against the property. You would not write a $25,000.00 bond on a defendant where the signer recently purchased a piece of property with little or no equity.

When accepting property as collateral, make sure that you are covered. This means, should the defendant "jump bail" on you, and your only alternative in recovering a loss is to foreclose on the property, you want to be sure that there is enough equity in the property to pay off your bond and any other expenses incurred. Generally, the longer a person has been in their property, the more equity that has been accumulated. These are the more favorable properties to accept when writing a bond.

9. PURCHASE PRICE OF PROPERTY

Knowing how much a person paid for their property, accompanied by the value of the property, and how much is owed on the property will give you a good idea of just how much equity is in the property. Once you know that there is adequate equity in a property to cover the bond that you are posting, you can go ahead and write the bond.

EXAMPLE: Arrestee in jail on $20,000.00 bond. Indemnitors paid $100,000.00 for their property eight years ago. They owe only $30,000.00 on the property today. Understand that the property has increased in value over the past eight years and the estimated value should be have appreciated a few thousand dollars. So this would be a good bond to write, because there is sufficient equity in the property to cover your bond.

10. BALANCE OWED ON PROPERTY

As you will see, the amount owed on the property, minus the value of the property, will give you the amount of equity that is in the property. Knowing this will tell you whether or not to write a bond. Use this formula to get equity:

Property Value
- Amount Owed (on property)
= Equity

11. FAIR MARKET VALUE OF PROPERTY

Many homeowners may not know the true value of the property being used as collateral. So you as a professional will derive an estimated value of the property pretty accurately by using the 11 Master Questions in your negotiations.

Getting your clients to answer these 11 Master Questions will become your meter in determining whether or not you will bail out a defendant. This little quiz will keep you in control of the conversation as well as get your clients to give up valuable information. If you come up with other worthwhile questions to ask your clients during the bail process, do so. There is no such thing as a dumb question in this business, especially when your money is on the line.

WORKING A BOND

Most bondsmen are satisfied with accepting only real property as collateral. These are the bondsmen who can afford the luxury of dictating what's acceptable at their office. This is good for you because everyone negotiating for bail will not own property. When negotiating a bail where real estate is not being used as 100% of the collateral, other valuable possessions should be considered.

Don't rule out anything of value. Working a bond boils down to asking questions and getting answers that will ultimately get you the collateral needed to help solve your client's problem.

COLLATERAL

The best collateral, other than real estate, is collateral that takes up the least amount of storage space and is valuable. You want collateral, that if necessary, can be sold expediently and at a discounted price. Consider the following items as alternative collateral if no real estate is involved:

1. Jewelry
2. Fur Coats
3. Color TV's - VCR - Camcorder
4. Stereo System - CD Player - Laser Disk
5. Automobile - Truck - Van - Motorcycle (With Pink slip or title proving ownership)
6. Stock Certificates

Also, don't rule out credit cards as a means of collateral. Many bail bondsmen are now accepting American Express, Visa and MasterCard as a form of cash collateral from clients.

When taking collateral such as the ones mentioned, make sure that it is secured safely and protected properly. Also, when taking any type of vehicle, you will need somewhere to store it. And I'm not talking about parking it on the street and moving it every other day.

The good thing about taking a vehicle as a means of collateral is that you can charge the customer storage fees. Even if you don't have a place to store the vehicle, you could easily arrange to have it stored at a garage or other type of safe facility and pass the charges on to the client.

CASE STUDY

A signer who has been on the job for five or more years and is employed at a well known company, wants to bail out a friend who also has favorable employment. No real estate is involved in the negotiations, and the bail is $1,000.00.

You could easily accept a diamond ring from the indemnitor, along with $500.00 cash. Of this $500.00 cash, $400.00 will be used as collateral and $100.00 for the premium (10% of the bail). The $400.00 and the ring would be returned to the indemnitor once the case was over and the bond exonerated. Although you may not be a jewelry expert or an appraiser, you could appraise the indemnitor who owns the jewelry. If the indemnitor looks shaky...then use your own good judgement.

SYNOPSIS

Many bondsmen would pass up this type of bond because no real estate is involved. You should always let the signers know exactly what you will accept as collateral, and nine times out of ten, they will try and get it. Also, try to get as much cash as you can on bonds written without real estate.

Do not be afraid to ask the indemnitor for all cash if they have no other acceptable collateral. The more cash collateral that you receive on a bond, the easier it will be for you to recover should you have to pay off a bond or have a defendant picked up due to a bail skip.

THE OFFENSE AND THE SERIOUSNESS

The offense will often indicate the seriousness of a crime as well as dictate what type of collateral will be needed to secure the bond. Take for instance, a 26 year old ex-felon, two time loser, in custody on a robbery charge.

He is an excellent candidate for the 3 Strikes Law which mandates a minimum of 25 years in prison. His bail is $100,000.00. You want to get strong collateral on this type of charge because this defendant is going straight back to prison if found guilty. And, if this defendant is not too anxious in returning to visit some of his ex-cellmates, he may decide to disappear and jump bail.

Now when this occurs, you'll looking at some trouble. This would be considered a bail forfeiture. This in effect would cause you and your insurance company to be responsible in paying off the entire bond of $100,000.00 if the defendant is not found in the required length of time. So you see, this is a prime reason for getting adequate collateral to cover yourself in all transactions, especially the larger ones.

Once you start writing bonds you will become familiar with criminal offenses and their seriousness. You will know what to look for and ask for when negotiating bail. As mentioned, on a robbery charge, the defendant is a candidate for prison. On a forgery rap, be aware of false documents, trust deeds, counterfeit money. etc., from the indemnitors and defendants.

These are just a few of the types of criminal offenses that you will be dealing with in this business. I recommend that you go to a legal bookstore in your area and purchase a criminal codes book. This will familiarize with the various misdemeanor and felony offenses.

COLLATERAL CHART

There are a combination of ways of working a bond using jewelry, furs, tv's, stereos and automobiles as collateral. The chart below will serve as a guide for you when accepting collateral other than real estate. This chart represents bail amounts up to

$2,500.00. It's a good idea to stay within this area if real estate is not used, because the stakes are not so high. When you start writing the larger bonds, the only thing you want as collateral is real estate or all cash.

BAIL AMOUNT	CASH COLLATERAL	PREMIUM	TOTAL CASH
$500.00	$250.00	$50.00	$300.00
$1,000.00	$500.00	$100.00	$600.00
$1,500.00	$800.00	$150.00	$950.00
$2,000.00	$1,000.00	$200.00	$1,200.00
$2,500.00	$1,250.00	$250.00	$1,500.00

(Remember, when negotiating a bond using this chart, you will also require the indemnitor to put up some jewelry, a fur coat, tv, stereo or auto along the cash collateral needed.)

Always use good judgement and discretion when writing a bond whether real estate is used or not. After you have been in the business for while you will be able to judge people on sight. This will enable you to determine a good risk from a bad one.

On occasions, you can accept just an indemnitor's signature alone, accompanied with some cash as collateral. Should you accept only a signature along with some cash as collateral, your main concern is the employment stability of the indemnitor as well as the defendant.

Make it a point to try and get at least two signers to sign when conducting this type of transaction. Your main criteria here will be the employment stability of the indemnitor(s) and defendant. You will want solid proof to verify employment up to at least five years or more on the job. That way, should you have to recoup any losses from a bail skip, you could garnish the wages of the indemnitors in order to collect. Always get valid identification such as:

1. Driver's License
2. Social Security Card

3. Work Identification Card
4. Recent Employment Check Stub
5. Utility Bill
6. Rent Receipt

RETURN OF COLLATERAL

Whenever you bail someone out of jail and the case is over and the bond exonerated, all collateral must be returned to the indemnitor(s).

If real property (real estate) was used as collateral, you must reconvey the property to the owners. Never reconvey the property to the indemnitors if there is a balance owed to you. Notify the parties involved that the case is over, and that they can pick up the reconveyance paper for their property.

If there are monies due from client, such as motion filing fees, etc., inform the indemnitors at this time. Have copies of motions, etc., as proof of money owed... so when the indemnitors come in to pick up their collateral, there won't be any surprises.

Just as real property has to be returned to the owners via reconveyance, personal property has to be returned to the owners also. When returning personal property, such as jewelry, tv sets, cash or automobiles to indemnitors, make sure that you have a system whereas the indemnitor must give you a 24 hour notice before retrieving any merchandise. This way you won't be sitting at the office with valuable merchandise.

Also, if an automobile is involved as collateral, make extra sure that all monies are paid before you go to the trouble of having the vehicle delivered to your office from the storage location. As mentioned, inform indemnitors of any other fees that are due, such as storage fees, etc.

CHAPTER 3:
BAIL BOND CATEGORIES

In the course of the day-to-day operations at a bail bond office there are basically three types of bail bonds written by agents. They include the standard bail bond, the federal bond and the appeal bond. We will also discuss a relative little used bond referred to as a "material witness bond".

THE STANDARD BOND

The standard bail bond is the most common bond used in the business. This is considered the bread and butter of the business because these are the ones you will write the most. Types of crimes will include, burglary, drug possession, drunk driving, traffic warrants, assault, joy riding, prostitution... you know, the type of crimes that are committed on a regularly basis.

This book deals exclusively with the standard bail bond, except when mentioned otherwise. So, when the word bond or bail bond appears through out this manual, you know that we are talking about a standard bail bond.

THE FEDERAL BOND

A federal bond is required when a defendant violates a federal law. Federal violations include such acts as bank robbery, mail fraud and theft, securities fraud, possessing illegal firearms, drug trafficking and income tax evasion, just to name a few.

Posting a federal bond is a little different from posting a standard bail bond due to the guidelines involved for this type of transaction. The premium on a federal bond is higher that the normal 10%, it can go up to 12% or more, depending on the locality.

Federal bonds can be complicated due to the nature of certain offenses. A person can be jailed for committing a federal offense and a state offense at the same time. Example: A defendant is in jail for robbing a liquor store, kidnapping an employee and taking that victim across state lines. It is up to the court to decide if this defendant will stand trial in both courts, federal and state.

Depending on the type of crime and the defendant involved, the state may drop all of the charges and let the federal authorities handle the prosecution, and vice versa. This is normally done to give the defendant the maximum sentence.

If the defendant has an attorney it's a good idea to let him get some of the specifics from the court before you put things into action. This way you won't be spending your wheels.

When requesting bail information for an arrestee on a federal charge, make sure that you contact the correct agency. The arrestee in a federal case is detained at a federal detention center, not in a city or county jail. Identification Numbers are used instead of Booking Numbers when requesting bail information on a federal arrestee. All information regarding the defendant such as charges, bail, case number, and collateral required comes from the federal court. The bail can be set in a number of ways; all cash, cash and property, several properties, corporate bond, etc, depending on the offense.

A bail forfeiture on a federal bond can mean serious trouble. Unlike the bail forfeiture on a standard bail bond, reinstatements are not so easy. Some bondsmen send a representative to court with the defendant on federal cases to make sure the defendant is on time for the appearance.

If a defendant appears late for a hearing on a federal case, there better be a verifiable life or death situation involved, otherwise the bond is forfeited and the defendant is remanded into custody. Also, an arrest warrant is issued immediately for the defendant who fails to appear on a federal case.

If the judge in a federal case declares a forfeiture of the bond, and refuses to reinstate the bond, the defendant must start all over again in the bail process. Oftentimes the judge will increase the bail as a form of punishment for the defendant.

Federal bonds are not as complicated as it may seem. The most important thing to remember when posting one for a client, is to remind him/her of the importance of being prompt for all appearances.

THE APPEAL BOND

When a defendant has been found guilty of an offense, and he/she faces jail time; or has been sentenced to jail or prison, the defendant, under certain conditions, can appeal the conviction and be re-tried. If the defendant is out on bond, whether a standard or federal bond, and appears in court for sentencing, this bond is exonerated. Once a defendant is sentenced on a case the bond is automatically exonerated and the case is over.

Now, if the defendant wants to appeal the sentence (jail time, etc.), and remain out of jail in order to fight the case on appeal, a new bond must be posted. This is an appeal bond. Actually, the appeal bond is a tool to keep the defendant out of jail, and at the same time gives the defendant a chance to come up with some new evidence to fight their case.

Appeal bonds can be expensive depending on the case. On any bond, and especially an appeal bond, the defendant must convince the judge he/she is not a flight risk factor. Meaning they will appear in court on time, when scheduled to do so, and are not appealing the case so that they can disappear or leave the country. The appeal bond is usually set according to the defendant's standing in the community and the nature of the offense.

A defendant will normally appeal a case if his/her attorney feels justice was not served to their satisfaction, or if the defendant is stalling for time, hoping a new judge will hear their case or some new evidence pops up in their favor.

MATERIAL WITNESS BOND

In the life of a bail bond business, you may never write a "material witness bond". Just so you'll be familiar with one, here's an example: Drug kingpin, Public Enemy #1 is arrested after an informant decides to testify and reveal evidence to the police. Public Enemy #1 has never been convicted of a crime because evidence and witnesses usually disappear before trial.

The material witness bond forces an individual (the informant) to remain in custody or to deposit a sum of money or a bond with the court adequate enough to insure his/her presence in order to testify at a forthcoming trial. The material witness bond serves as a legal device for witnesses, to ensure that they appear in court. It also keeps the prosecution's case strong with evidence that would otherwise be put in jeopardy.

TRAFFIC WARRANTS

Traffic warrants come under the Vehicle Code violations (V.C.). These violations include such offenses as speeding, reckless driving, driving with no license or registration, running a stop sign or red light, no license plates on vehicle, making an illegal U turn, just to name a few.

An arrest warrant is issued when a defendant fails to appear in court to face these Vehicle Code violations. Normally a fine is imposed, and on many occasions jail time, depending on the number of infractions and the seriousness.

If a person is arrested on a traffic warrant, he/she goes immediately to jail. There are no ifs, ands or buts. There are several options available to a defendant faced with a traffic warrant arrest: (1) They can pay the full amount of the traffic warrant(s) and be released after they are booked at the police station; (2) They can remain in custody and appear in court the following business day to faces charges on the warrants. At this time the defendant will be sentenced, (with the possibility of being released with time served in jail, or incur additional time in jail depending on the charges); or (3) They can contact a bail bondsman and post bail on all of the warrants.

If the defendant decides to post bail on the traffic warrants, he/she will still have to appear in court and face paying a fine or serve time in jail. Many bondsmen do not write bonds for traffic warrants because they are a pain in the you know what, because of the paperwork. And by the same token, other bondsmen make this their bread and butter business.

The average bondsman will not write a traffic warrant bond unless it is associated with another crime, (such as a defendant being arrested on a drug charge and he/she has traffic warrants also), or the bonds total more than $1,000.00 or more in traffic warrants. New bondsmen in the business can attract new clientele by catering to writing traffic warrants for their clients.

CASE STUDY

Defendant is arrested after a high speed chase from the local police. Upon checking the defendant for possible warrants, it is discovered that the following traffic warrants are outstanding for the defendant's arrest: 13355 V.C., (driving under a suspended driver's license); 10851(a) V.C., (auto theft) and 23152(a) V.C., (driving under the influence (of drugs or alcohol).

SYNOPSIS

If the defendant contacts a bail bondsman in order to gain his/her freedom, the bail bondsman must write three (3) separate bonds (in addition to the new charges) to complete this transaction: (1) a bond for the 13355 V.C., driving under a suspended driver's license, (2) a bond for the 10851(a) V.C., auto theft, and (3) a bond for the 23152(a) V.C., driving under the influence of drugs or alcohol. Just think if this person had eight (8) traffic warrants. Is it worth it?

SPECIAL CIRCUMSTANCES

In many criminal cases, whether federal or state, certain conditions may be required of the defendant if he/she wishes to remain out on bail. Also, bail is usually high when such conditions are set in play. These special circumstances normally place a subtle and austere handicap on the defendant.

The majority of defendants who are out on bail with special conditions are usually prohibited from leaving his/her home between certain hours. Usually if the defendant is employed, he/she is allowed to go to work and return straight home.

Some conditions require the defendant to wear a radio-type leg device that monitors the defendant's whereabouts 24 hours a day. If the judge, federal prosecutor or magistrate finds out that the defendant removed, tried to remove the device, or left the area of surveillance, bail is usually revoked immediately unless there is a very good reason.

Certain high profile criminals who have special restrictions placed on them are limited in participating in their profession. Take the case of a professional football player accused of drug trafficking. He must phone his probation officer twice a week as well as meet him twice a month. Also, a condition of his bail is that he cannot travel outside the Central District of California. This type of condition prohibits him from traveling with his team on games outside of the prescribed area. Restrictions like these are costly.

In one city, a celebrity musician accused of assault, among other things, wished to remain out on bail rather than go to jail. The conditions of his bail was that he would have to wear a monitored anklet 24 hours a day and he could not leave his home between the hours of 9:00 pm and 6:00 am. This cost him dearly, because most concerts begin and end between these times.

Usually if a defendant shows improvement, like following the bail conditions without any problems, and staying out of trouble, his/her attorney can ask the judge for a modification of the bail conditions. In order to get a modification of bail restrictions, an attorney must petition the court stating what restrictions need modifying. If time is of the essence, a ruling date is also requested by the attorney. When special conditions are modified on a defendant, bail can increase or decrease depending on the case.

CHAPTER 4: LONGEVITY IN THE BUSINESS

Longevity in any business means change...changing with the times and staying in front of the competition. If you are doing business in the 21st century, but your equipment, work habits, office environment and marketing techniques are outdated, your business won't be around long.

The veterans in the bail bond industry who have been around 20 or 30 years know what it takes to stay in this business. Hard work and long hours are two of the main ingredients that pave the way to success and longevity for the professional bondsman.

STAYING POWER

The art of staying in the bail bond business is being able to recover should you take a loss. Bail forfeitures put more bondsmen out of business than anything else. The thing about a bail forfeiture is that if you do not take care of it in time - you have to pay. Your main concern when writing a bond is being able to recover.

When negotiating a bond for a client, you should ask yourself "How will I recover should this defendant jump bail?" If you have done your homework and asked the signer the 11 Master Questions, your risks should be very minimal. Qualifying the indemnitor as well as the defendant in a thorough manner will put you in a position to recover easily should a bail forfeiture occur.

Remember that if you are dealing with decent, honest people as a whole, you have a chance. First of all, a decent person does not want to risk losing hard earned property, or other collateral that is put up in a defendant's behalf. Secondly, the decent client will help you find the defendant should he/she happen to disappear.

The term "decent people" is used because there are some people that you will come in contact with who are not decent. They will come to you with the intention of "beating you", so to speak. By this I mean lying, bringing false documents, forged papers, deeds, and identification, etc. These are the customers you want to be aware of. Surely if they are out in the streets everyday trying to beat the system and making a living at it, just think what they'll try on you.

You have your protection against these types of individuals by using the 11 Master Questions. If a person does not qualify after you have asked the 11 Master Questions, then the bond is not worth writing. The secret to this business is being able to recover. Yes, you will get bail forfeitures, it goes with the business. But being able to recover makes this business fun and rewarding.

CASE STUDY

Bondsman #1 writes a million dollars worth of business in one year. He runs his business in a sloppy manner, taking inadequate collateral and not qualifying his clients. The majority of his money is spent on paying off bail forfeitures and hiring bounty hunters to track down defendants. He's out of business in no time.

Now on the other hand, take Bondsman #2 who also writes a million dollars in business. But he runs a tight ship. He accepts only good, strong collateral and he thoroughly qualifies his clients. The money he has made is his to keep. He will be in a position to expand his business and open up other offices.

SYNOPSIS

The bottom line is, "Always take enough collateral to recover any losses that should occur". This is the key to staying in the bail bond business.

CHECKING BAIL FORFEITURES

As mentioned earlier, bail forfeitures put more bondsmen out of business than anything. To avoid this pitfall, the easiest thing to do is to have a system to check your bail forfeitures. A simple procedure for doing this is as follows:

1. When you receive a bail forfeiture notice from the court, pull the defendant's file immediately.

2. Using a calendar, determine the 180th day, which is the final day in which to surrender defendant.

3. Contact the indemnitor(s) right away to find out if they are aware that the defendant failed to appear in court.

4. Arrange to have defendant come into the office and sign bail motion papers so bond can be reinstated immediately.

5. If defendant does not appear within a week or so without a good reason, contact a bounty hunter, put pressure on the indemnitors and prepare on foreclose on property.

6. Inform defendant and indemnitor(s) of possible fees involved (i.e. filing fees, attorney fees and court costs) in having bond reinstated. Also explain to them the seriousness of a bail forfeiture.

7. File motion with court where forfeiture originated and give indemnitor(s) new court date and time. If you have an attorney who normally represents your office in filing motions, inform all parties concerned and describe attorney to them. Have defendant check in with the court clerk on date of hearing and notify them that he/she is present and will be represented by an attorney. Inform defendant to wait for the attorney who will file the motion to have bond reinstated.

8. Once bond is reinstated, check docket sheets for updates on the case to see if defendant was released on O.R., etc.

CASE STUDY

Bondsman receives a notice of bail forfeiture from the court for a defendant on a drug charge. The bondsman makes an attempt to contact the defendant regarding the matter. Defendant is not available so bondsman talks with defendant's parents (indemnitor) regarding court appearance. Indemnitors swear on a stack of bibles that their daughter (defendant) went to court.

Bondsman prepares motion papers to have bond reinstated. Also found out thru the courts that defendant did appear in court, but was late. Motion is filed to have bond reinstated.

SYNOPSIS

Never, never take the defendant nor the indemnitor(s) word on anything when it comes to bail forfeitures. The only person you believe is what the court says. Defendant and his/her entire family may say defendant was in court. So what! If the courts say it's a bail forfeiture, then it's a bail forfeiture. And the only way to correct this, is to file a motion to have bond reinstated.

FILING MOTIONS

In the course of doing business, you will from time to time file various motions with the courts. You can appear in court personally and file the motion, or you can have an attorney on retainer who's primary job is to meet the defendant(s) in court and file the motion in behalf of your bail bond agency.

There are many types of motions that will keep you in business. The most common ones include motions to have bond reinstated or exonerated and motion to have time tolled on bond forfeiture date.

The motion to have a bond "exonerated" will be one of your major tools in closing many bail forfeiture cases. When you find out that a defendant you bailed out is back in custody, whether under the name you bailed him/her out on or some alias, filing a motion to have your bond exonerated is the ticket. Each motion that you file in order to have a bond exonerated is different, depending on the case. (See Chapter 8)

Another tool that will help keep you in business is the motion the have "time tolled" on bond forfeiture date. This type of motion is really a stalling tactic in an attempt to get more time from the court so you can locate a bail skip. This tool can save you thousands of dollars if the forfeiture time is up and the court allows you more time in bringing the defendant back into court. (See Chapter 8)

CHECKING BOND STATUS

In order to stay in business, a monthly visit to the courthouse to check bond status is necessary. The status of a case on which you wrote a bond for, is kept on what's called a "docket sheet". This sheet has the defendant's name, booking number, bond number and case number.

It has a chronological history of the defendant, starting from when he was arrested, when a bond was posted, up until the time the defendant was sentenced or if there was a bail forfeiture.

The docket sheet has a record of the defendant's appearances in court and non-appearances. By retrieving a copy of the docket sheet you will know the status of many of your cases. Also in doing this, you can have many cases exonerated faster instead of waiting for the courts to notify you.

Whenever using a docket sheet as proof of status concerning a case, always get a certified copy of the docket sheet as well as a certified copy of the bond. The courts may charge a small fee for this service, but it saves you in the long run.

Also, when an indemnitor claims that a case is over and exonerated, have him/her go to the court and get a certified copy of the docket sheet and bond as proof. This will save you a trip to the courthouse.

BOUNTY HUNTERS

A good Bounty Hunter or Bail Skip Retrieving Agency is worth their weight in gold. When the word bounty hunter is mentioned, some of you may think of a hired gunman from the frontier days who tracks down criminals. Well, today's bounty hunters operate in a similar fashion, they track down bail jumpers, for a fee.

When dealing with bounty hunters, call on them as your last resort. Use up all of your resources first: Contact the indemnitor(s) to inquire as to the whereabouts of a defendant. If the defendant was employed, call his/her place of employment. Check with the county jail in your city, (in Louisiana, the Parish Prison) to see if the defendant is back in custody. If you run into a brick wall after utilizing these avenues, then bring a bounty hunter into the picture.

BOUNTY HUNTER FEES

Bounty hunters are not cheap. They charge a fee to find and bring in a defendant on a bail forfeiture. Their fees may range anywhere from 10% up to 50% of the bail amount. Some bounty hunters charge a flat fee on all cases. While others may charge according to the expenses involved and how important it is to the bondsman to have the bail jumper back in custody.

STRAIGHT PICKUP

A "straight pickup" is easy money for a bounty hunter. This is the type of capture when the bondsman knows the exact location of a bail jumper as supplied via indemnitors, reliable informers, etc. The bondsman will supply the bounty hunter with all of the necessary information to place the bail jumper back into custody.

The bounty hunter will be supplied with all of the information on the bail skip including name, height, weight, complete physical description and a picture if possible. Also, known hang outs such as bars, motels and gambling houses are given to the bounty hunter.

The bounty hunter will apprehend the bail jumper and surrender him/her to jail, enabling you to get out of paying the bail forfeiture. There is little work done because the bounty hunter goes straight to the target for the pick up.

STAKE OUT

When you have no leads in finding a bail jumper, a bounty hunter may have to "stake out" a neighborhood or areas that are known hang outs of the bail jumper. The bounty hunter will wait patiently, often in dangerous places to surprise a bail jumper.

Many bounty hunters, armed with the picture of a bail jumper will walk through the neighborhood, ask questions regarding the whereabouts of the target, hoping that someone will be a good samaritan and lead him to the bail jumper.

Stake outs can be long and tiresome because it may take days or even weeks for the target bail jumper to show up. Stake outs work well on bail jumpers who have limited family and limited resources because sooner or later time takes its toll.

It is not uncommon for bounty hunters to go to another city or state in order to bring back a fugitive from justice. When this occurs you will be charged accordingly. That is why fees can range from 10% up to 50% of the bail amount.

CASE STUDY

Bondsman posts bond for a defendant on a $50,000.00 bail. The defendant fails to appear in court and a bail forfeiture is received regarding defendant's failure to appear. Although good, strong collateral was placed for the bond, the indemnitors cannot be located. The bondsman contacts a bounty hunter.

A bounty hunter will normally charge 10% on a straight pickup, which would be $5,000.00 to bring in this bail jumper. If the bounty hunter has other expenses, such as travel, extra help, etc., the fee could easily jump to 50%, especially if time is of the essence.

SYNOPSIS

When all else fails, call in the bounty hunters...especially when you cannot contact the indemnitors. Why sweat it out worrying about it. As long as sufficient collateral is put for a bond, the bondsman is always in the clear of coming out of his/her pocket to pay for a bail forfeiture.

The good thing about hiring a bounty hunter is that whatever fees are incurred to bring in a defendant, those fees are passed on to the indemnitor. Keep this in mind, whatever you have to pay a bounty hunter is a whole lot cheaper than paying the full amount to the court.

Also, once the indemnitor is aware that all fees incurred to bring in the defendant will be coming out of their pockets, they will assist you in finding the defendant. Unless, of course they just don't care and may even want the defendant to remain missing.

An indemnitor who has pledged his home as collateral would be glad to pay a paltry bounty hunter's retrieving fee rather than having to pay off an entire bond and risk losing everything that he/she may own.

Quite a few bail bondsmen do their own bounty hunting and make extra money rather than hire someone else to do this job. A bounty hunter service is another business that you can operate out of your bail bond agency and make good money also.

CHAPTER 5: YOUR FUTURE

Your future in the bail bond business will depend totally on you and your efforts. How well you treat your clients and build new business will determine your future as a bondsman.

Finding new clients to bail out of jail looks bright also. Because as long as teenagers are growing up to become adults, there will always be a future for the professional bondsman. Although crime reports show a decline in crimes committed by adults, crimes committed by teenagers has skyrocketed. In the next five to ten years we can expect to see a new surge in crime based on reports from the U. S. Department of Justice regarding teenage crime.

In Los Angeles, many bondsmen are venturing into auto sales, real estate, pawn brokerage, as well as opening offices in other nearby communities to insure a more profitable future.

These type of businesses seem to compliment a bail bond business simply because of the collateral that many bondsmen end up possessing. Once you get started and going good in the business, you'll know what direction you'd like to expand, so your future can be rewarding

BACKBONE OF THE BUSINESS

The accounts receivable is the backbone of any business where you have customer accounts or extend credit. Just how do you build up a good accounts receivable file? By extending credit to your clients, that's how. This is an area that may be inconceivable to many bondsmen. Most bondsmen refuse to extend credit to their customers - and at the same time they lose good clients.

You must exercise extreme caution and use the utmost discretion when extending credit in this business, because some people forget that they owe you once the defendant is released. They do not believe in paying back debts the old fashion way, whereas your word is your bond, and if you promise to pay on a designated day, payment is received.

There are bondsmen in this business who have clients that owe them, and although the client(s) may be on fixed incomes, they manage to pay on time, always. The key to extending credit to certain clients is "Keep Good Records". Keep a separate file for your accounts receivable customers, because you want to make sure all debts are paid before you extend future credit. The accounts receivable file can prove to be your money tree during a slow period because you will always have someone that owes you money.

When establishing your accounts receivable file, extend credit only to your Class A customers. These are the clients that have good strong collateral such a nice home, business or job. You have a good chance of recovering should a bail forfeiture occur when extending credit to these types.

As long as you take in enough collateral to cover yourself, you still can recover should a client fail to meet their obligations. Always get a verbal commitment from the indemnitor and write it down. Get an agreement as to when the first payment will start and when the balance will be paid off. Let the indemnitor choose the time table and the amount that they are comfortable with. (As long as it is within reason).

CASE STUDY

Indemnitors want to bail out their son on a $25,000.00 bond for forgery. Indemnitors own property and have excellent employment history. The premium is 10%, which amounts to $2,500.00. The indemnitors have only $1,500.00. The bondsman could easily arrange to have them pay installments of $100.00 to $200.00 a month until the balance of $1,000.00 is paid off, with no sweat.

SYNOPSIS

This would be a perfect transaction for an accounts receivable file because you would have excellent collateral (the property) should the indemnitors fail to meet their credit obligations. Also the fact that the indemnitors and defendant have good employment. And as long as clients have some type of income, they will try and meet their obligations with the bondsman because they never know when they will need him again.

Once you have established a good accounts receivable file, never press the clients about payments. Experience has shown that once you extend credit to someone in this business, they never forget it. They will tell others what a nice bondsman you are and the professional type of business that you operate.

By no means this is implying not to collect what is owed to you. The way to collect on past due accounts is to give the client a call one day after a payment was due. Let the client know that you took their word that a payment would be made (say yesterday). If they do not have the amount due, for reasons unknown, tell them to see what they can get and contact you regarding the amount.

This is the key - if you do not hear from the client who owes, wait one or two weeks, then call the client and remind him/her about the past due account. They will respect you for this because you have not hounded or harassed them. And by now they should have some type of money for you. They will have a guilty feeling also, knowing that you met your obligation in getting a friend or loved one out of jail, and they have not paid you for your services.

Usually if a phone call does not work, due to disconnection, or party never home, send a threatening letter regarding foreclosure of property, forfeiture of collateral or wage garnishment. This will surely get results.

THE REAL DEAL

Most people look at a bail bondsman as a dubious, cold-hearted type of person who fattens his pockets at the expense of people in trouble with the law. He merely sits behind a desk, collects money and get people out of jail. The latter is partly true; but the real part of this business is the work that goes unnoticed, the work that others don't see.

There are countless forms and documents to deal with, the daily, weekly and monthly reports that have to be completed. There are motions to be filed, bail jumpers to track down, bounty hunters to pay, debts to collect, and the numerous visits to courthouses to check on the deposition and status the bonds. It goes on and on.

The real deal in this business is being able to survive. And the only way to survive in this business is to be in a position to recover by staying on top of everything. One bad bond written can put a bondsman out of business. It's the small everyday things that others don't see that keep a bondsman in business.

A BONDSMAN NEVER SLEEPS

A bondsman is a bondsman 24 hours a day, 7 days a week, and then some. This is not nine to five gig where you clock in at a certain time and leave at a certain time. If you are having a good day writing bonds, you will work two, three days straight, getting little or no sleep.

During the riots in Los Angeles of 1992, there were bondsmen who worked day and night for days at a time with little or no sleep, because business was so brisk. Yes, there will be days when business seems non-stop. It's these type of days that compensate the bondsman for slow periods in the business.

COMPLETING THE PUZZLE

This business can be compared to putting together a gigantic puzzle. It starts with a phone call or an office visit from someone wanting to bail out a friend or relative. Your first step is to call the jail and get bail information regarding the person in jail. You take an application to qualify the parties involved. After qualifying the indemnitor(s) regarding collateral and employment, you write a bond, post it, and the defendant is released.

If the case goes smooth and the defendant makes all court appearances and sentenced, the bond is exonerated. Once you have proof that the case if over, collateral is returned to indemnitor.

If the case does not go smoothly and you get a bail forfeiture, you have to act on it and straighten out the matter. There are phone calls to be made and people to see. A bounty hunter may have to brought into the picture in order to find the defendant. And if the defendant is discovered to be back in jail, motions have to be filed in order to have the bond exonerated.

This is the puzzle that you are putting together. Every case is different and every puzzle is different. That's what make this business fun, exciting, educational and rewarding.

BUILDING YOUR BUSINESS

Just like anything else, building your bail bond business will undoubtedly take time. When just starting out, advertisement and word of mouth will be the main vehicle for generating customers.

Once you build your business to a certain degree, you will have regular clients who seem to just stay in trouble. These regular clients in turn will be a source of future referrals.

ADVERTISEMENT

The average person who needs to bail someone out of jail will rely on advertisement in the yellow pages of a local telephone book or ask a friend to recommend a bail bondsman. A good creative ad in the yellow pages will attract new customers to you. Your advertisement will serve as your image.

See how other bondsmen are advertising in the yellow pages; take two or three of the eye-catching ads and create your own. Be imaginative and add some of your own personal touch and you should come up with a pretty good ad. You should also place a small ad in your neighborhood newspaper for additional exposure.

Passing out your business card is another way of generating new customers and building your business. Business cards are inexpensive and you should make it a habit of giving a card to everyone that you come in contact with, friends, relatives, strangers, everyone. When you are at the market, barber shop, cleaners, liquor store, car wash, and any other place that you may visit frequently, pass out your business cards.

The concept behind passing out business cards is that the people who you give a card to may not need your services at that particular time, but if and when the time does come, and a bondsman is needed - you may be the one that is called or referred to for help. In this business, everyone is a potential client.

DEALING WITH ATTORNEYS

Another way to build your business is to contact attorneys in your area and let them know that you are available. Use extreme caution here, because soliciting attorneys for business is prohibited in some states, California being one.

Just as you will have regular clients who just can't stay out of jail, so do attorneys. Attorneys are not in the bail bond business and they do not specialize in negotiating bail or posting bonds. They will need your services one time or another to bail out one of their clients.

Attorneys are excellent contacts for appeal bonds. Take for example: an attorney's client is found guilty of a charge. Instead of starting a prison sentence, the client chooses to appeal the conviction due to some technicality during the trial. If a Judge approves the appeal, a bondsman will be needed to post the bond. You could easily become the personal bondsman to several attorneys in your area. As mentioned throughout this book, use discretion at all times and check all local laws.

JAILERS

The local jails are prime sites to consider when building your business. Be aware that in some states it is unlawful for a bondsman to solicit business at a jail.

The best way to get a referral from the local jails is to be friendly with the jailers on duty when you are posting a bond. If you carry yourself in a professional manner, you could easily strike up a conversation and tell them who you are and they will remember you.

Although jail personnel are not allowed to refer prisoners to a bondsman, your name just may pop up. Most jailers have enough finesse to mention a name to an inmate seeking a bondsman without making it look like a referral.

During the holiday season many bondsmen have Christmas parties and invite jail personnel to visit their office to meet the staff. Also, policemen are always sponsoring some type of function, like the Policemen's Ball, an excellent place to meet jail personnel.

AFFILIATIONS

Your church, social club or other affiliations would be excellent spots to advertise your business. You could offer to bail out members and their family with little or no collateral, depending on their credentials. Discretion is the key. Remember, as long as you put yourself in a position to recover if there is a bail forfeiture, you have nothing to lose.

MONEY IN THE BANK

The bail bond business has a built-in nest egg and protection fund for the bondsman that know how to stay in business. This nest egg can grow to enormous size depending on the number of "good bonds" you write in the lifetime of your business.

"Good bonds" are bonds that do not result in bail forfeitures that have to be paid off by you or your insurance company. This is your money in the bank. The nest-egg, referred in the bail bond business as the Build-Up Fund/Reserve Account is generally set up to protect you and the insurance company from risk, in the event of a bail forfeiture that has to be paid off.

THE BUILD-UP FUND

The Build-Up Fund is an account set up for the bondsman by the insurance company that he/she will be writing bonds for. Every time a bond is written, a percentage of the premium goes into this special fund.

This is how it works: Say you've been in business for about five years and you write a bond for $5,000.00, whereas you took real estate as collateral. The defendant you bailed out disappears, and you receive a bail forfeiture notice from the court. You cannot get in touch with the indemnitor(s) who pledged the collateral, so you foreclose on the property.

During the foreclosure process you discover that there are other liens on the property ahead of you, and it is unlikely that you will receive a dime for the trust deed in your possession. The forfeiture time is near and you are faced with paying the court $5,000.00, plus any penalties and fees, if the defendant is not found in the required length of time.

You hire a bounty hunter, place a wanted picture of the defendant in the neighborhood newspaper, the whole sha-bang... the defendant is not found and you come up empty handed... and you don't have $5,000.00 cash on hand, what do you do? You would contact the general agent or manager at the insurance company that you are writing bonds for and explain the problem.

The money that you have accumulated via of your build up fund can be used to pay off the forfeiture. So you see, this is an excellent account to bail you out, should you be faced with the unfortunate situation of paying off a bail forfeiture

If you negotiate wisely and take in good collateral, rarely will you have to touch your build up fund to pay off a bail forfeiture. Just think, after writing good bonds with no forfeitures for several years, you will have a nice nest egg built up.

There are bondsmen right now, who have at least one million dollars in their build up fund account. They built this fortune over a period of time, with hard work. And just as soon as all of the cases are over and exonerated in their files, these bondsmen are entitled to the full amount in the account.

Actually, the build up fund serves as a retirement-type nest egg and a means of rewarding the bondsman who writes good bonds. When you retire from this business you could easily walk away with a small fortune. That sure beats a fake gold watch you may receive upon retirement from a 9 to 5. Be sure to have your general agent explain the build up fund to you regarding the insurance company's procedures and guidelines.

Most bondsmen never retire, they just relinquish control of their office operations to one of their trained agents or family members who will run the office just as he/she would. This enables (the owner) to continue to have money deposited in the build up fund account even though he/she may be out golfing, fishing or whatever, because every time the office writes a bond, a percentage of the premium still goes into the build up fund account.

This is just about one of the easiest jobs in the world once you get established. Everything will become a regular routine and habit; qualifying clients, writing bonds, checking on bail forfeitures and docket sheets, filing motions and reports. You will become familiar with the different types of criminal offenses, the penal code, the vehicle code, collateral you will and won't accept and protecting yourself against bail forfeitures.

You will always have money in the bank as long as teenagers are turning into adults. Crime will always be a thorn in society and regardless of the circumstances, when a person goes to jail, they want one thing — and that is to get out. And as a professional bondsman, you hold the key.

CHAPTER 6: SOLID ADVICE

In every business there are risks as well as rewards, the bail bond business in no different. One advantage of the bail bond business is that the rewards outnumber the risks involved.

RISKS

The biggest risk in the bail bond business will be writing a bond without verifying or taking adequate collateral. This is a very true statement because should you write a bond that results in a bail forfeiture, and the defendant is not found in the required time, you have to pay. You know this, right?. And if you have several of these occurrences, financial disaster awaits.

BAIL FORFEITURES

The most unfortunate aspect of this business is paying off bail forfeitures. A bail forfeiture itself is not serious, because the majority of them have easy remedies. The only time a bail forfeiture poses a threat is when the defendant is not found in the required time. Throughout this manual attempts have been made to provide you with guidelines to help minimize the risks involved. And by minimizing your risks, you maximize your rewards.

REWARDS

The rewards of being a professional bondsman definitely out number the risks. This is a very lucrative business. On a good day you can make anywhere from ten to twenty five thousand dollars cash in less than an hour.

CELEBRITY CASES

Take the O. J. Simpson case in Los Angeles, California, June 1994. You remember his friend, Al Cowlings, who's daring efforts to keep O. J. from committing suicide, was charged with aiding an abetting a fugitive. Mr. Cowlings bail was set at $250,000.00 for his participation. He and whoever, had to come up with $25,000.00 cash (10% of the bail) and some serious collateral to get out of jail. The bondsman who wrote that bond is probably still smiling.

Take John Gotti, who has had numerous arrests and few convictions, but has always managed to bail out of jail before the ink dried on his fingerprint card. You can bet his bail bondsman dreaded the day he was convicted and hauled off to jail to serve twenty some odd years in prison.

Take this for instance, ten members of an international drug ring are arrested and the bail for each defendant range from $100,000.00 up to 1 million dollars. You get the business to bail out four of the defendants (accepting good strong collateral, of course). You are looking to make at least $40,000.00, in one shot, and this is not unusual. You cannot expect these type of bonds everyday - once a year is doing good.

BREAD AND BUTTER

Once you get started in this business you will see that your rewards will come from your bread and butter bonds... the ones consisting of $10,000.00 and less. As you gain experience in the business you will see that the bread and butter bonds come every day and the big ones will come in cycles.

One month you may write two or three $50,000.00 bonds and the next month none. In the long run it all evens out. How many people do you know, excluding sports figures, that make $5,000 to $10,000 in just thirty minutes? (The time it takes to write and post a bond at a jail).

You are about to enter a profession that can provide you with a stable, secure income and can expand to your desires. You do not need a college degree nor do you have to be genius in order to get into this profession. All you have to do is study and pass a simple test, which you can do, and that's it. The bail bond business is practically recession and inflation proof. Whether good times or bad, the bail bond business seems to always attract new customers.

TIPS FOR SUCCESS

I. Always be suspicious of an indemnitor who calls from a pay phone and insists that they do not have a telephone. Make sure that these type of clients have more than adequate collateral. Because should there be a bail forfeiture, you'll have no way to contact the indemnitor.

II. Take an extra bond or two with you when you go to a jail and bail someone out. Bail information can change while enroute to the jail as well as having been given incorrect bail information by a jailer.

III. In large metropolitan areas like Los Angeles, when you post a bond for a defendant, it is a good policy to call back to the jail in an hour or so to see if the bond was received and if the defendant was released. This is for your protection and credibility, because the people who put up the money for the defendant will be very concerned regarding the release of this person. So when the indemnitor does call, checking on the release of the defendant, simply tell them "The bond has been posted and the defendant is being processed for release". This keeps you on top of the situation.

IV. Whenever a surprise charge comes up in the course of bailing someone out of jail, such as a traffic warrant, notify the indemnitor(s) immediately. Usually the traffic warrant will appear after a bond has been posted for defendant to be released. The defendant will not be released until the traffic warrant has been paid or a bond posted for the warrant. Inform the indemnitor of the new charges so they can determine if they want to pay cash at the jail to cover the traffic warrant, have a bond posted for the warrant or leave the defendant in jail until after the warrant(s) have cleared.

V. For every charge that a defendant is in custody on, a bond must be posted. Example: Defendant arrested and charged as follows — attempted murder, possession of controlled substance, and a traffic warrant for speeding. As you can see, this defendant has three different charges. The bail for the attempted murder charge may be $25,000; the bail for the possession charge may be $10,000 and the traffic warrant may be $1,000. You have a bond total of $36,000, for which you will write a bond for each individual amount corresponding with the offense.

These are only a few tips that will save you much time and trouble as a professional bondsman. They come from many years of experience. Although they may not seem important now, but let the situation arise and then weigh their significance.

CHAPTER 7: LICENSING PREPARATION

There are a few procedures necessary in preparing for your bail bonds license. Since you will be handling large sums of money, dealing with various divisions in the judicial as well as the criminal system, adequate preparation is imperative.

The following chapter will give you an overview of the requirements necessary to acquire of your bail agent's license.

APPLYING FOR BAIL AGENT'S LICENSE

Applying for a bail agent's license is a very simple procedure. First of all, just about everything that you need will be supplied to you by the Department of Insurance in your area.

One suggestion before you start on your quest to become a bail bondsman is to have some type of financial back-up. Most insurance companies will require that you place a cash deposit in a reserve account until your business is self-sustaining. If you have bad credit be prepared to offer the surety company addition collateral, maybe the equity in some real estate or even cash. As mention before, each surety company has it's own rules and regulations.

PREPARATION FOR THE EXAM

Preparing for the bail agent's exam is as easy as preparing for any other exam. This manual provides you with some helpful information to study as well as some possible questions to expect. (See the California Administrative Code). Keep in mind that this information presented before you is adapted for the state of California bail agent's exam, as each state has different material.

The examination for the bail agent's exam is composed of a written test of job-relevant abilities and a questionnaire dealing with various aspects of the business. By combining these measures, the examination provides a comprehensive index of your knowledge relating to your probable job success. It is very important that you study the types of sample questions included in this manual before the examination. It is advisable to do this repeatedly over a period of time to become familiar with the item types.

PURPOSE OF THE EXAM

The written bail agent's exam is designed to measure: (1) the ability to understand language and procedures in the bail bond business, and (2) the ability of candidates to comprehend guidelines, rules and regulations governing the bail bond industry.

TIME LIMIT

In each part of the test, a reasonable amount of time is included for the careful reading of the instructions. Be sure to use this time well. Each part of the test has a definite time limit. There is enough time for most people to answer each question. Nonetheless, some questions may be a little more difficult than others.

Do not spend an excessive amount of time on one question to the detriment of your total test performance. You can always go back to a skipped question if you finish a part of the test before the time limit for that part is over.

ANSWERING THE QUESTIONS

First, read each question very carefully. Then, read the alternative responses given and if you know the correct answer, darken the corresponding space in the answer booklet or answer sheet. If a question appears especially difficult, you may choose to leave it and return to it later before time is called. If, after the test, you think you did not answer all the questions correctly, do not be discouraged. No applicant is expected to answer every question correctly.

POSSIBLE TEST QUESTIONS

Listed on the following page are some possible questions to expect on the examination. The questions selected are similar to the questions you will find on the actual exam, in terms of difficulty and form. In general, the test questions deal with topics related to the Administrative Code governing bail bonds which you would be likely to encounter in the performance as a bail agent. Remember, however, that knowledge of any legal subject matter is NOT required to answer the questions correctly. (Answers are provided following the exam along with the explanation taken from the California Administrative Code).

BAIL AGENTS EXAM: POTENTIAL QUESTIONS

1. Which of the following are true of a bail agent?
   a. A bail agent can be an active member of the State Bar.
   b. A bail agent is one who conducts, or supervises the conduct of bail business pursuant to contract with surety insurer.
   c. Must be 21 or more years of age.
   d. Can bail anyone out of jail, no matter what the charge.

2. A person actually detained or subject to detention in custody whose release may lawfully be effected by bail is:
   a. Bail permittee
   b. Bail solicitor
   c. Bail agent
   d. Arrestee

3. Every bail agent or permittee shall conduct his bail business:
   a. As an individual
   b. As a member of a partnership as provided in Section 2061.
   c. As an employee of another bail agent or permittee as provided in Section 2062.
   d. All of the above.

4. Before using a fictitious name or style, it must be filed with and approved by the commissioner in writing.
   a. True
   b. False

5. A bail agent can enter into an agreement or arrangement, with any person in advance guaranteeing bail will be furnished for an offense.
   a. True
   b. False

6. A bail agent may not solicit business for bail in prison, jail, or other place of detention.
   a. True
   b. False

7. A bail agent shall solicit bail in accordance with Section 2079.5 and from:
    - I. An arrestee.
    - II. The arrestee's attorney.
    - III. A Jailer.
    - IV. An adult member of the arrestee's immediate family

    a. I and III
    b. I, II and IV
    c. II and III
    d. III and IV

8. A bail agent who receives collateral can co-mingle the collateral with his own funds.

    a. If it's approved by the commissioner.
    b. Only by written authorization from the depositor.
    c. As long as the depositor is not aware of it.
    d. Never.

9. If collateral received is in excess of the bail forfeiture, such excess shall:

    a. Become property of the bail agent.
    b. Shall be split between the bail agent and depositor.
    c. Shall be returned to the depositor.
    d. Shall be deposited into a reserve account for future bail forfeitures.

10. After the final completion of all parts of a bail transaction, a bail licensee may destroy records pertaining to such transactions:

    a. After 5 years
    b. After 1 year
    c. After 180 days
    d. After 2 years

BAIL AGENTS EXAM: ANSWERS TO POTENTIAL QUESTIONS

1. b Whenever the term article "bail" or "transaction of bail" includes undertaking of bail and "bail bond" as that term is defined in Insurance Code Section 1800.4, including the activities in respect to execution or delivery of undertakings of bail of any person, whether designated "general agent" or otherwise, who conducts, or supervises the conduct of bail business pursuant to contract with surety insurer. (2054.2)

2. d As used in this article "arrestee" means any person actually detained or subject to detention in custody whose release may lawfully be effected by bail. (2054.5)

3. d Every bail agent or permittee shall conduct his bail business: (a) as an individual; (b) as a member of a partnership as provided in Section 2061; (c) as an employee of another bail agent or permittee as provided in Section 2062. (2065)

4. a Prior to its use, a fictitious name or style must be: (a) filed with and approved by the commissioner in writing; (b) filed with the county clerk of all counties in which the user thereof maintains an office for the transaction of bail or in which he contemplates the active solicitation of bail under such fictitious name or style. (2066.3)

5. b No bail licensee shall enter into an agreement or arrangement with any person, which agreement or arrangement has for its purpose the guaranteeing or assuring such person or any other person in advance of the commission of any offense that bail will be furnished to such person or any other person when and if such person any other is arrested, nor shall any bail licensee perform any act which will encourage any person to violate the law. (2070)

6. a Except as provided in Sections 2079 and 2079.5, no bail licensee shall solicit any person for bail in prison, jail, or other place of detention of persons court or public institution connected with the administration of justice; or in the halls or corridors adjacent thereto; provided that a bail licensee may, in such halls, corridors or in other rooms or areas where not prohibited by local rule or ordinance transact bail with persons specified in Section 2079 who have prior transaction, requested his services. (2074)

7. b No bail licensee shall solicit bail except in accordance with Section 2079.5 and from: (a) An arrestee; (b) The arrestee's attorney; (c) An adult member of the arrestee's immediate family. (2079)

8. b Any bail licensee who receives collateral in connection with a bail transaction shall receive such collateral in a fiduciary capacity, and prior to any forfeiture of bail shall keep it separate and apart from any other funds or assets of such licensee. (2088)

9. c If collateral received is in excess of the bail forfeiture, such excess shall be returned to the depositor immediately upon the application of the collateral to the forfeiture; subject, however, to any claim for unpaid premium or charges as provided in Section 2081. (2089)

10. a Five years after the final completion of all parts of a bail transaction, a bail licensee may destroy records pertaining to such transactions. (2104)

CALIFORNIA ADMINISTRATIVE CODE

Title 10, Chapter 5, Subchapter 1,
California Administrative Code
Article 2. Bail Transactions

PRELIMINARY

2053. Application; Construction. This article as amended is applicable to all applications for licenses filed after the effective date of such amendments, to all transactions or severable portions thereof occurring thereafter and to the keeping of all records pertaining to such transactions or severable portions thereof. All such applications filed prior thereto and all trans-actions or severable portions thereof occurring prior thereto and the keeping of records pertaining thereto shall be governed by the provisions of this article which were in effect prior to such date. Insofar as the provisions of this article are substantially the same as the provisions of this article restatements and continuations thereof and not as new provisions.

2053.1 Past Violations; Power of Commissioner. Insofar as the provisions of this article are new provisions, their promulgation shall not preclude the commissioner from taking such action as is permitted by law for acts or omissions which occurred prior to the effective date of these amendments.

2054. Definitions; Applications of Insurance Code. Insofar as they are applicable, the definitions contained in the General Provisions and in Chapter 7, Part 2, Division 1 of the Insurance Code are applicable to this article.

2054.1. "Bail License"; "Bail Licensee"; Terms Defined. As used in this article "bail license" includes all licenses specified in Section 1801 of the Insurance Code and "bail licensee" the holders thereof whether on a permanent or temporary basis and whether as individuals or as members of a partnership.

2054.2. "Bail Agent" or "Permittee" Includes Co-partners. Whenever the term "bail agent or permittee" is used in this article, such term includes the members of a partnership of bail agents or permittees if applicable.

2054.3. "Bail"; "Transaction of Bail"; Terms Defined. As used in this article "bail" or "transaction of bail" includes undertakings of bail and "bail bond" as that term is defined in Insurance Code Section 1800.4, including the activities in respect to execution or delivery of undertakings of bail of any person, whether designated "general agent" or otherwise, who conducts, or supervises the conduct of bail business pursuant to contract with a surety insurer.

2054.4. Payment of Commissions; Unlawful Rebates; Prohibited. No person may receive commission on bail or the transaction of bail as defined in section 2054.3 unless he holds a bail license as defined in Section 2054.1. No bail licensee shall pay or allow in any manner, directly or indirectly, to any person who is not also a bail licensee any commission or other valuable consideration on or in connection with a bail transaction. This section shall not prohibit payments by a bail licensee to an unlicensed person of charges by such person for services of the kind specified in Section 2081(c) and (d).

2054.5. "Arrestee" Defined. As used in this article "arrestee" means any person actually detained or subject to detention in custody whose release may lawfully be effected by bail.

2045.6. Notices; Time for Filing. Whenever any provision for this article requires that notice be given to or that filing be made with the commissioner a specified period of time before a matter may lawfully be used or an event lawfully occur, such period of time may be reduced by the commissioner at the request of the licensee if good cause is shown therefor.

2054.7. Notice of Noncompliance; Request and Hearing. Whenever pursuant to any provision of this article the commissioner gives notice to any person that such person may not establish a particular relationship or perform a particular act, such person shall upon written request therefor filed within 10 days of said notice be granted a hearing within 60 days following the date of such notice on the issues of noncompliance specified in such notice. Whenever pursuant to the provisions of this article the commissioner gives notice to any person to discontinue within a specified time a particular established relationship or the performance of a particular act, such person shall upon written request therefor filed within 10 days of said notice be granted a hearing on the issues of noncompliance specified in such notice which shall be held at least 10 days prior to the date specified in the notice as the date such person shall discontinue the relationship or the act.

LICENSE REGULATIONS

2055. Applications; Forms. All applications for original or renewal bail licenses shall be on forms furnished by the commissioner. All applicants for such licenses and all bail licensees shall furnish such supplementary information and supporting statements as the commissioner may require.

2056. License Qualifications. An original bail license shall not be issued to any person unless he:

(a) Is a California resident and has been such for a period of two years immediately preceding issuance of the license.

(b) Satisfies the commissioner that he is a person of good business reputation and of good general reputation in:

(1) The community in which he intends to principally engage in the transaction of bail, or,

(2) The community or communities in which he formally resided, if he has not been resident of the community in which he intends to principally engage in the transaction of bail for a sufficient period of time to establish such reputation.

(c) Is 18 or more years of age.

2057. Prohibited Associations. An original or renewal bail license shall not be issued to any person nor shall it be kept in force if he is:

(a) Regularly or frequently employed by or associated with:

(1) A court of law in respect to its exercise of its criminal jurisdiction, if any,

(2) A public law enforcement agency possessing the power of arrest and detention of persons suspected of violating the law in the specific terms of the statutes establishing and governing the agency.

(b) A private patrol operator.

(c) An active member of the State Bar of California.

(d) Associate of persons of bad general or bad business reputation, or criminals, except to the extent that such association is required in the transaction of bail with such persons.

(e) In case the associations defined in (d) above are only with persons related to the licensee or applicant by blood or marriage, on good cause shown the commissioner may issue the license applied for or a restricted license, or may revoke an existing license and issue in lieu thereof a restricted license.

2058. License; Prior Prohibited Associations. An unrestricted original bail license shall not be issued to any person if within the two-year period immediately prior to his application a license would not have been issued to him for any of the reasons specified in Section 2057(a); but a restricted bail license may be issued to such person if he presents evidence satisfactory to the commissioner that his bail business will be conducted in a county other than any county wherein he was employed by or associated with a court of law or law enforcement agency; or that such business will be conducted only in part of the same county so remote from the place of his prior employment that such employment will have no affect on his conduct of his bail business.

2059. Solicitor; Other Licenses Prohibited. A person licensed as a bail solicitor may not at the same time be licensed as:

(a) A bail agent.

(b) A bail permittee.

(c) A bail solicitor for more that one employer unless all such employers are partners, in which event he shall be licensed as a solicitor for all partners.

TRANSACTION OF BAIL THROUGH PARTNERSHIPS AND EMPLOYEES

2060. Only natural persons may be issued a bail license.

2061. Transaction as Partners; Notices. Two or more bail agents or permittees desiring to transact bail as partners shall file with the commissioner the written statement required by Section 2061.2 at least 10 days prior to so transacting, except as provided by Section 2061.3.

2061.1. Partners; Individual Licensing; Rebating. Each partner shall be licensed individually as a bail agent or permittee, or both, and every partner shall be licensed in the same capacity or capacities as the other members of the partnership so that all partners will be licensed in the same capacity or capacities; except the commissioner may permit the inclusion of an unlicensed partner if evidence is presented satisfactory to him that such unlicensed partner will have no functions, duties or responsibilities involving the actual conduct, supervision or transaction of the bail business.

2061.2. <u>Co-partners; Filing Individual Statements</u>. A written statement subscribed by each partner shall be filed with the commissioner setting forth:

(a) The nature of all businesses conducted or intended to be conducted by the partnership.

(b) The location of the principal place of conduct of the bail business of the partnership and of all other places for the conduct of such business.

(c) The proportion of ownership of each member of the partnership.

(d) An agreement to immediately notify the commissioner of any change in the membership of the partnership or of the matters set forth in (a) to (c) hereof.

2061.3. <u>Change in Partnership; Notices</u>. Upon any change in the membership of the partnership whether through death, dissolution, addition, deletion, or otherwise, or upon the revocation of the license of any partner, the survivors or successors to the bail business, if they are to act as a partnership, shall file a new statement pursuant to Section 2061.2 and shall be subject to the requirements of Section 2061.1. If the change in membership arises through the death or revocation of the license of a partner in a partnership of three or more persons whose partnership agreement provides for continuation of the partnership by the survivors, such survivors may continue to transact bail as a partnership until the expiration of such reasonable period of time as may be specified in any notice which may be sent by the commissioner pursuant to Section 2054.7.

2061.4. <u>Co-partnership Suspension; Prohibitions</u>. If the license of any partner is suspended such partner may not engage in the transaction of bail nor may he receive any commission on, or profit derived from, such transactions entered into by other persons during the period of suspension.

2061.5. <u>Co-partnership; Disciplinary Action for Act of One Partner</u>. The licenses of each member of a partnership are subject to suspension or revocation for the failure of the partnership or of any member of the partnership to comply with all laws and rules governing or regulating the conduct of the bail business or acts incidental thereto if such failure occurred with his express or implied knowledge, consent, ratification or collusion.

2062. <u>Licensed Employees; Notice of Employment</u>. A bail agent or permittee or a partnership of bail agents or permittees desiring to employ another person licensed as a bail agent or permittee for the purpose of assisting him in his bail business shall file with the commissioner a written statement as required by Section 2062.2 at least 10 days prior to such employment. If prior to the expiration of such 10-day period the commissioner gives notice to the prospective employer specifying wherein such employment would be contrary to any provision of this article or any law relating to bail, such person shall not be employed. If after such 10-day period and after the establishment of the employer-employee relationship the commissioner gives notice to such employer and to such employee specifying wherein the continued employer-employee relationship would be contrary to any provision of this article or any law relating to bail, they shall discontinue such relationship within such reasonable time as the commissioner may prescribe.

2062.1. Employee; Licensed in Same Capacity as Employer. Each such employee (employed pursuant to Section 2062) shall be licensed in the same capacity or capacities as the employing bail licensee or bail licensees.

2062.2. Employment; Written Notices. A written statement subscribed by the employee and each such employee (employed pursuant to Section 2062) shall be filed with the commissioner setting forth:

(a) The fact of employment.

(b) The location of the place of business from which the employee will normally transact bail.

(c) The basis of compensation of the employee and if such compensation is to be more than $1,000.00 per month the amount thereof.

(d) An agreement to immediately notify the commissioner in writing of any change in the matters set forth in (a) to (c) hereof.

2063. Licensed and Unlicensed Employees; Effect. Sections 2063.1 to 2063.2, inclusive, apply to each employee of a bail agent or permittee whether or not such employee is licensed as a bail agent, permittee or solicitor if such employee performs any duties connected with the transaction of bail by his employer.

2063.1. Employer Supervision; Disciplinary Action. An employing bail agent or permittee shall exercise a reasonable degree of supervision over his employees and make a reasonable effort to keep informed of their acts as his employees. Failure of the employer to exercise such supervision resulting in the violation of law or these regulations by the employee may result in disciplinary action against the employer.

2063.2. Branch Offices. A bail licensee (i.e., the owner, a partner or a licensed employee) shall be in charge, as his usual and customary place of business, of each branch office.
2063.3. Solicitor; Transactions and Conduct. A bail solicitor shall not conduct a bail business or transact bail under any name or at any address other than that of his employer, nor shall he use any forms or documents in connection with a bail transaction other than those of his employer.

CONDUCT OF BAIL LICENSEES

2064. Bail Licensees; Capacity and Conduct. Every bail licensee shall conduct his business in such a manner that the public and those dealing with him shall be aware of the capacity in which he is acting, and if he transacts bail both as an employee and as an individual or any other dual capacity, each such transaction shall be so conducted that the public and those dealing with him shall not be confused as to the capacity in which he acts.

2065. Business in Specified Capacities Only and Notices. Every bail agent or permittee shall conduct his bail business:

(a) As an individual;

(b) As a member of a partnership as provided in Section 2061;

(c) As an employee of another bail agent or permittee as provided in Section 2062;

(d) As the temporary associate of another bail agent or permittee in the joint transaction of bail if such temporary association is limited to a single transaction or to a series of related transactions;

(e) As the temporary conductor of the bail business of another bail agent or permittee during a period of his temporary absence; or

(f) In any other lawful manner provided written notice is filed with the commissioner by the bail licensee at least 10 days prior to his so conducting his bail business setting forth full details of the manner in which the business will be conducted and the names of all persons, if any, to be associated with him. If prior to the expiration of such 10-day period the commissioner gives notice to such bail licensee specifying wherein the intended conduct of the business would be contrary to any provision of this article or any law relating to bail, such bail licensee shall not so conduct his business. If after such 10-day period the commissioner gives notice to such bail licensee specifying wherein the continued conduct of his bail business would be contrary to any provision of this article or any law relating to bail, he shall discontinue to so conduct his business within such reasonable time as the commissioner may prescribe.

2066. Business in Own Name. Except as provided in Section 1724.5 of the Insurance Code and the commissioner's regulations promulgated thereunder (Section 2050 and following of Title 10 of the California Administrative Code) and Sections 2066.2, 2066.3, 2066.4 hereof, every bail licensee shall do business in his own name.
2066.1. Using Employer's Name. Every bail agent and permittee employed by another bail agent or permittee pursuant to Section 2062 and acting as such and every bail solicitor shall do business only in the natural name or fictitious name, if any, of his employer.

2066.2. Using Predecessor's Name. The permission under Section 1724.5 of the Insurance Code to use a predecessor's name in case a bail agent or permittee purchases or succeeds to the bail business of another bail agent or permittee is applicable only where the business so purchased or succeeded to was a bona fide business which the predecessor or predecessors had actively conducted as a bail business for at least 5 consecutive years.

2066.3. Fictitious Names; Filing; Similar Names. Prior to its use, a fictitious name or style must be;

(a) Filed with and approved by the commissioner in writing.

(b) Filed with the county clerk of all counties in which the user thereof maintains an office for the transaction of bail or in which he contemplates the active solicitation of bail under such fictitious name or style.

(c) Worded in compliance with the requirements of Section 1724.2 of the Insurance Code and the regulations of the commissioner promulgated under authority thereof (Sections 2050 and following of Title 10 of the California Administrative Code).

2066.4. Disapproval of Fictitious Name. If the commissioner gives notice to a bail agent or permittee specifying wherein the continued use of a fictitious name would be in violation of any of the provisions of the Insurance Code or this Article, such bail agent or permittee shall discontinue the use of such fictitious name subject to such extension of time as the commissioner may prescribe pursuant to the provisions of Section 1724.5 of the Insurance Code.

2066.5. Advertising of Fictitious Names. All advertising or telephone listings in the yellow pages of telephone directories shall contain the true name of the licensee(s) who owns it with equal prominence with that of the fictitious name, so that there will be no

indication that another separate business exists when in fact, the ownership is the same.
2067. Misrepresenting Capacity; Authority. No bail licensee shall directly or indirectly represent that he is a fidelity or surety insurer or that he has the authority or powers of a bail permittee, bail agent, or bail solicitor unless he is licensed as such; nor shall he misrepresent his authority or power to act on behalf of a surety insurer; nor shall he advertise his bail business in the yellow pages of the telephone directory under "Surety" or "Fidelity".

2068. Transactions by Unlicensed Persons; Prohibitions. No bail licensee shall directly or indirectly permit any person on his behalf to solicit or negotiate undertakings of bail or bail bonds or to effect undertakings of bail or to issue or deliver bail bonds unless such person is properly licensed by the commissioner to perform such acts, even though such person acts in a purely mechanical or ministerial manner or renders his services gratuitously. This section shall not prevent a bail agent or permittee from using the mail, or any messenger or delivery service used by the public generally, to file executed undertakings of bail or deliver bail bonds, nor shall it prevent such filing or such delivery by the attorney or other agent of the arrestee. No person in the employment of the licensee shall act as an agent of the arrestee in the performance of any of the acts specified herein.

2069. Confidential Communications; Information. No bail licensee shall disclose or reveal any information coming into his possession or to his knowledge concerning an impending arrest or detention of a person by a law enforcing agency, except in accordance with the lawful inquiry of a law enforcement or judicial officer, unless such information is a matter of public record or knowledge.

2070. Agreements for Bail Before Arrest; Prohibited. No bail licensee shall enter into an agreement or arrangement with any person, which agreement or arrangement has for its purpose the guaranteeing or assuring such person or any other person in advance of the commission of any offense that bail will be furnished to such person or any other person when and if such person or any other person is arrested, nor shall any bail licensee perform any act which will encourage any person to violate the law.

2071. Suggesting or Recommending Attorney; Prohibited. No bail licensee shall in any manner, directly or indirectly, suggest the name of or recommend any attorney to any arrestee or person purporting to act for or represent an arrestee.

2072. Acting for Attorney; Prohibited. No bail licensee shall receive, accept or collect for, or transmit to, any attorney any money or other item of value for attorney's fee, costs or any other purpose on behalf of an arrestee or any other person with whom bail is negotiated. Any bail licensee who is lawfully holding any money or other item of value as collateral may, however, upon the release of such collateral, honor an assignment thereof to an attorney if the licensee took no part in the negotiation of such assignment. No bail licensee shall furnish forms for or otherwise aid in such assignment.

2073. Preparation of Writ of Habeas Corpus; Prohibited. No bail licensee or his employees shall prepare, make, or assist in any manner in the preparing, making or filing of a petition for a writ of habeas corpus for or on behalf of an arrestee. Such licensee or his employees may, however, without charge and in accordance with the specific directions of the attorney of the arrestee, perform such mechanical and ministerial acts as will assist such attorney in preparing or making such petition.

2074. Unlawful Solicitations; Place. Except as provided in Sections 2079 and 2079.5, no bail licensee shall solicit any person for bail in prison, jail, or other place of detention of persons, court or public institution connected with the administration of justice; or in the halls or corridors adjacent thereto; provided that a bail licensee may, in such halls, corridors or in other rooms or areas where not prohibited by local rule or ordinance transact bail with persons specified in Section 2079 who have prior to transaction, requested his services.

2075. Regulations of Public Authority; Compliance. Every bail licensee shall fully comply with every rule, regulation or ordinance issued by a proper public authority governing the conduct of persons in or about any prison, jail or other place of detention of persons, court or public institution connected with the administration of justice. This section shall not be construed to authorize any act constituting a violation of any other section of this article which is done pursuant to any rule, regulation or ordinance that is merely permissive in its nature.

2076. Informing or Notifying of Arrests; Prohibitions. No bail licensee shall, for any purpose, directly or indirectly, enter into an arrangement of any kind or have any understanding with a law enforcement officer, newspaper employee, messenger service or any of its employees, a trusty in a jail, or other person incarcerated in a jail, or with any other persons, to inform or notify any licensee (except in direct answer to a question relating to the public records concerning a specific person named by the licensees in the request for information), directly or indirectly, of:

(a) The existence of a criminal complaint;

(b) The fact of an arrest; or

(c) The fact that an arrest of any person is impending or contemplated.

(d) Any information pertaining to the matters set forth in (a) to (c) hereof or the persons involved therein.

2077. Fictitious Communications. No bail licensee shall, directly or indirectly transmit or cause to be transmitted to himself or to any other person a communication authorizing said licensee or any other person to solicit or negotiate bail which is a fictitious communication or which is from a person other than a person whom he may lawfully solicit bail pursuant to Section 2079 or with whom he may lawfully negotiate bail pursuant to Section 2080. No such communication shall, at any time or in any manner, be used directly or indirectly as an aid in securing information concerning a person confined in a jail, prison or other place of detention or for the purpose of visiting an arrestee therein, or for any other purpose.

2077.1. Identification Card. Every bail licensee shall keep in his possession an identification card issued to him by the commissioner and shall, upon request, show it to any person with whom he transacts bail. He shall not permit any person other than himself to use his identification for any purpose. The identification card shall be returned to the commissioner immediately upon the termination of all of the holder's bail licenses.

2078. Gifts Prohibited. No bail licensee shall give, directly or indirectly, any gift of any kind to any public official or employee of any governmental agency who has duties, functions or responsibilities in respect to the administration of justice or a place wherein detention of persons charged with crime may occur, or to a prisoner in any jail or place of detention. Items of nominal value which are distributed generally for the purpose of advertising shall not be considered gifts for the purpose of this article, except if given to prisoners or persons directly in charge of prisoners in their place of detention; nor shall this article prevent the customary giving of gifts to relatives by blood or marriage. But nothing in this Section shall be construed to justify any rebate or bribe.

2079. Soliciting of Bail; Persons. No bail licensee shall solicit bail except in accordance with Section 2079.5 and from:

(a) An arrestee;

(b) The arrestee's attorney;

(c) An adult member of the arrestee's immediate family; or

(d) Such other person as the arrestee shall specifically designate in writing. Such designation shall be signed by the arrestee before the solicitation, unless prohibited by the rules, regulations or ordinances governing the place of imprisonment. If so prohibited, it may signed after release of the arrestee to ratify a previous oral designation made by him.

2079.1 Solicitation of Arrestee; Hours. Any solicitation of an arrestee himself pursuant to Section 2079(a) shall be only after a bona fide request for bail services has been received from the arrestee or from a person specified in Section 2079(b) or (c). Any solicitation of a person specified in section 2079(c) or (d) shall be only between the hours of 7 o'clock a.m., and 11 o'clock p.m., unless the bail licensee is directly and specifically authorized in writing by the arrestee or the arrestee's attorney to make such solicitation at some other specified time.

2080. Negotiation of Bail; Persons. No bail licensee shall negotiate concerning bail, except with:

(a) A person specified in Section 2079;

(b) Any other person who without previous solicitation on the part of the bail licensee has requested his services.

2081. Collection and Charges Permitted. No bail licensee shall, in any bail transaction or in connection therewith, directly or indirectly, charge or collect money or other valuable consideration from any person except for the following purposes:

(a) To pay the premium at the rates established by the insurer and set forth on the undertaking of bail or to pay the charges for the bail bond filed in connection with such transaction at the rates filed in accordance with Section 2094.

(b) To provide collateral.

(c) To reimburse himself for actual, necessary and reasonable expenses incurred in connection with the individual bail transaction, including but not limited to:

(1) Guard fees after the first 12 hours following release of an arrestee on bail;

(2) Notary fees, recording fees, necessary long distance phone expenses (i.e., telephone calls billed by the telephone company as "long distance", but not for those for which "message unit" charges only are made); telegram charges, travel expenses and verification of collateral outside of the county where the bail was arranged; a reasonable posting fee charged by a licensee operating in a county other than that where the bail was arranged; providing that no charge shall be made for travel from the licensee's office to post bail in an area where the licensee advertises in the yellow pages of the telephone directory unless the advertisement specifically so states. Such travel charges, when permitted, shall not exceed the amount

allowed to be taken as a travel expense for income tax purposes under the federal Internal Revenue Code and Regulations thereunder, or the amount allowed by the State of California to be claimed for mileage by its employees, whichever the licensee chooses.

(d) To reimburse himself for actual reasonable and necessary expenses incurred and caused by a breach by the arrestee on any of the terms of the written agreement under which and pursuant to which the undertaking of bail or the bail bond was written. Such reimbursement may not exceed the penal amount of such undertaking or bond and may include a reasonable charge for the services of the licensee, his employees, partners, or other persons associated with him in the particular transaction of bail.

(e) If a forfeiture of bail occurs and it is not set aside, the expenses under (c) and (d) of this Section which are incurred within 180 days of such forfeiture may be charged in addition to the amount of such forfeiture.

2082. Prohibited Service Charges. Except to the extent permitted by Section 2081(c), (d), and (e), no bail licensee shall make any charges for his services in a bail transaction in addition to the premium on an undertaking of bail or the charge for a bail bond at the rates filed in accordance with Section 2094.

2083. Written Statements of Bail Transactions; Contents; Delivery. Every bail licensee shall, at the time of obtaining the release of an arrestee on bail or immediately thereafter, deliver to such arrestee or, if the negotiations concerning the bail were not with the arrestee, to the principal person with whom such negotiations were had, a numbered document containing the following information:

(a) If an undertaking of bail, the name of the surety insurer.

(b) The name and address of the bail licensee.

(c) The name of the arrestee.

(d) The date of release of the arrestee.

(e) The date, time and place of the arrestee's required appearance.

(f) The amount of bail.

(g) The offenses with which the arrestee is charged.

(h) The premium if an undertaking of bail, or the charge if a bail bond.

(i) An itemization of all actual expenses described in Section 2081(c) and (d), supported by vouchers and receipts, or true copies thereof.

(j) The total amount of all charges.

(k) The amount received on account.

(l) The unpaid balance, if any.

(m) A description of and receipt for any collateral received and a statement of any conditions relating thereto including a copy of any written agreement executed in connection therewith.

2083.1. <u>Same; Additional Statements</u>. If, after the release of an arrestee, additional expenses are incurred or charges made, the bail licensee shall immediately deliver to the person specified in Section 2083 an additional numbered document containing the information required by Section 2083(h), (i), (j), (k) and (l).

2084. <u>Guarantor Agreements; Delivery; Notices</u>. All guarantor agreements shall be in writing, or reduced to writing as soon as possible after consummation. If any person acts as a guarantor, a copy of the guarantor's agreement shall be delivered to him promptly upon his execution thereof. No bail licensee shall enforce any such agreement without disclosing to the guarantor all collateral held by such licensee indemnifying the bond to which the agreement relates, and the identify of all other guarantors thereof, if any.

2086. <u>Undertakings of Bail; Delivery; Compliance</u>. No bail licensee shall deliver an undertaking of bail which does not comply with all of the provisions of Section 381 of the Insurance Code.

2087. <u>Waiver of Rights of Guarantor; Prohibited</u>. No bail licensee shall require the waiver by a depositor of collateral or by a guarantor of any right he might have or thereafter acquire in connection with any bail transaction. No bail licensee shall require or accept in connection with any bail transaction waiver of defense, confession of judgement, or other agreement impairing the right of the person with whom the bail is negotiated or any depositor of collateral or guarantor to a determination of his rights in a civil court.

2088. Collateral; Fiduciary Relation. Any bail licensee who receives collateral in connection with a bail transaction shall receive such collateral in a fiduciary capacity, and prior to any forfeiture of bail shall keep it separate and apart from any other funds or assets of such licensee.

2088.1 Collateral; Custody Thereof. If pursuant to his agreement or contract of agency employment or partnership any bail licensee is or may be required, or in fact does, transfer collateral to another bail licensee, general agent, or surety insurer, such recipient of said collateral shall hold it in the same fiduciary capacity as the licensee, return it, and otherwise handle it in conformity with Section 2088 through 2089, both inclusive, hereof. Such collateral shall only be transferred to another licensee or to a surety insurer holding a certificate of authority in California and said collateral shall not be removed from this state.

2088.2 Return of Collateral. Any collateral received shall be returned to the person who deposited it with the bail licensee or to any assignee of such person, other than the bail licensee or his representative, as soon as he is advised that the obligation, the satisfaction of which was secured by the collateral, is discharged. It is the duty of the bail licensee or surety insurer to determine promptly whether such obligation has been discharged upon request for return of the collateral by the person depositing it or by his assignee. If the collateral was deposited to secure the obligation of a bond, it shall be returned immediately upon the entry of any order by an authorized official by virtue of which liability under the bond is terminated. If any licensee or surety insurer which has custody of the collateral fails to take promptly any action necessary to secure the termination of such liability, he shall return such collateral immediately upon accrual of any right to secure an order of termination of liability. If such collateral was deposited as security for unpaid premium or charges and if such premium or charges remained unpaid at the time of exoneration and after demand therefor been made by the licensee or surety insurer which has custody of the collateral, the collateral other than cash may be levied upon in the manner provided by law and the proceeds of such collateral may be applied to the amount of such unpaid premium or charges.

2088.3. Real Property as Collateral. If a bail licensee receives as collateral in a bail transaction, whether in his own or on another's behalf, any document which conveys title to real property, such document shall state on its face that it is executed as part of a security transaction. If such document is recorded, a reconveyance of such property executed in such a manner that it may be recorded shall be delivered by the responsible bail licensee or surety insurer to the person executing the original conveyance or to his heirs, legal representative or successor in interest immediately upon such responsible party learning of the satisfaction of the obligation secured; and it is the duty of such responsible party to determine promptly whether such obligation has been discharged upon request for return of the collateral by the person entitled thereto.

2089. Return of Excess Collateral on Forfeiture. If collateral received is in excess of the bail forfeiture, such excess shall be returned to the depositor immediately upon the application of the collateral to the forfeiture; subject, however, to any claim for unpaid premium or charges as provided in Section 2081.

2090. Surrender of Arrestee to Custody; Return of Premium. No bail licensee shall surrender an arrestee to custody prior to the time specified in the undertaking of bail or the bail bond for the appearance of the arrestee, or prior to any other occasion when the presence of the arrestee in court is lawfully required, without returning all premium paid for such undertaking or bond; except that when as the result of judicial action, information concealed or misrepresented by the arrestee or other reasonable cause, any one of which was material to the hazard assumed, and the licensee can show that the hazard was substantially increased, then the bail licensee may retain incurred out of pocket expenses permitted to be charged by Section 2081(c) and (d). The surrender of an arrestee who is again in custody for an offense for which a penalty greater than that for the original offense may not be imposed, or his surrender at the request of the guarantor shall never, in and of themselves, be considered to be reasonable cause for surrender, and the case of any surrender under such circumstances, and no actual and substantial increase in hazard can be shown by the licensee, all premiums received and incurred expenses shall be returned. Compliance with an Order of the Court made pursuant to Section 1300(b) of the Penal Code shall be compliance with this Section; and a licensee at the time of any surrender of an arrestee prior to the time specified in the undertaking of bail shall inform such arrestee of his rights under said Section 1300(b) to petition the Court for a ruling as to return of premium.

2091. Forfeitures; Misrepresentations. No bail licensee shall make any misleading or untrue representation to a court or to a pubic official for the purpose of avoiding or preventing a forfeiture of bail or of having set aside a forfeiture which has occurred, or for the release of an arrestee on his own recognizance after bail has once been placed by the licensee. A copy of all written representations made by or on behalf of a bail licensee for such purpose shall be kept as provided in Section 2098, unless such representations are filed by an official as a public record.

2092. Interrogations; Licensee Must Answer. Every bail licensee must truthfully answer any question asked him by the commissioner or his representative about his bail transactions or matters relating to the conduct of his bail business, subject only to his lawful constitutional rights against self-incrimination.

FILINGS AND RECORDS

2094. Filing Schedule of Charges. Every bail permittee shall file with the commissioner a schedule of charges to be made for bail. He shall also file with the commissioner any change in such charges at least five days prior to the effective date thereof. Such charges and changes so filed are public records.

2094.1. Rates Chargeable. No bail permittee shall issue or deliver a bail bond except at the rates most recently filed with the commissioner in accordance with Section 2094.

2094.2. Filing of Charges; Difference in Rates. If a person is licensed as both a bail agent and an bail permittee or licensed in either capacity but conducting his bail business under an agreement with a person licensed in the other capacity, any filing made pursuant to Section 2094 shall state all differences between the premiums charged for undertakings of bail and the charges made for bail bonds and the reasons therefor. If there is any such difference and if for his own convenience a bail licensee shall substitute or cause to be substituted one type of obligation for the other, he shall do so without additional premium or charge. Such substitution without additional premium or charge may not be used as a device or means of avoiding compliance with Section 2094 or with Chapter 9, Part 2, Division 1 of the Insurance Code.

2905. Filings; Necessary Notices. Every bail licensee shall promptly file with the commissioner the following:

(a) If conducting business as a partnership pursuant to Section 2061, the written statement required by Section 2061.2 and any modification thereof.

(b) If the relationship of a bail agent or permittee employed by another bail agent or permittee or a partnership of bail agents or permittees exist as set forth in Section 2062:

(1) The written statement to the commissioner required by Section 2062.2;

(2) The written notice of any change as required by Section 2062.2(d).

(c) The written notice required by Section 2065(f) if applicable to such licensee.

(d) The written notice required by Section 2066.4(a) of any fictitious name or style used pursuant to Section 2066.4.

(e) A written notice of any changes made in any of the licensee's business addresses.

(f) A complete list of all persons employed by the licensee who aid him in any way in the conduct of his bail business setting forth for each employee the full name, duties and basis of compensation, and if such compensation is to be over $1,000 per month the amount thereof.

(g) A notice containing the same information as that required by (f) above for each new employee.

(h) A notice of termination of the employment of any employee and, if the reason therefor was any act or conduct by the employee which would in the opinion of the employer indicate an unfitness to transact bail, a full statement of such reason.

(i) A notice within 10 days after service upon him of the filing of:

(1) Any criminal suit;

(2) Any action at law against him or of any judgement against him which arises out of his transaction of the bail business or the transaction of bail.

(j) A written notice within five days after making any arrangement of any kind to obtain money, securities or other assets to use directly or indirectly in the bail business, giving the name of the person with whom such arrangements have been made, the amount of money or value of other assets involved, the date of the transaction and the details of the arrangement.

(k) A copy, or a reference to copies already filed and which he will use, of all forms or documents which the licensee intends to use regularly or frequently in connection with his bail transactions, including:

(1) The document to be delivered to the arrestee or other person containing the information required by Section 2083;

(2) The form of any receipt for or agreement relating to collateral used pursuant to Section 2083(m);

(3) The document to be delivered to the arrestee or other person containing the information required by Section 2083.5;

(4) The form of guarantor's agreement referred to in Section 2084;

(5) The form of original communication referred to in Section 2097(a);

(6) The form or original application referred to in Section 2097(b); and

(7) Any other form or document.

2096. Improper Forms; Notice. If the commissioner finds that any form or document, the filing of which is required by Section 2095(k), is misleading or contrary to any provision of this article or any law relating to bail, he shall notify the bail licensee specifying wherein such form or document is misleading or contrary to any provision of this article or any law relating to bail. Thereafter such bail licensee may not use such form or document. If such notification is not given to such licensee within 30 days after the filing of such form or document, the commissioner shall prescribe a reasonable time after which such form or document may not be used.

2097. Documents; Retention of Originals or Duplicates by Licensee. Every bail licensee shall retain in his records the original duplicate original of the following:

(a) Any written request received by him from an arrestee or person action on his behalf which resulted in the posting of bail by such licensee.

(b) The application for bail signed by the arrestee or person negotiating bail on his behalf.

2098, Documents; Retention of Copies by Licensee. If a bail licensee has arranged for the posting of bail, he shall in each case retain in his records a copy of the following documents:

(a) The document or documents furnishing the arrestee or person negotiating bail on his behalf with the information required by Section 2083.

(b) The collateral receipt or any form of agreement relating thereto described in Section 2083(m).

(c) A document listing additional charges required by Section 2083.5.

(d) Any written representation made to a court or a public official with respect to the matters dealt with in Section 2091.

(e) Any guarantor's agreement.

(f) All documents signed by the arrestee or any person with whom bail is negotiated, the originals of which are not retained by the licensee.

(g) All documents delivered to the arrestee or any person with whom bail is negotiated.

2099. Documents; Tender to Arrestee or Representative. Every bail licensee shall tender a copy of any document which is executed by any person with whom bail is negotiated to such person at the time of the execution thereof.

2100. Necessary Record; Open to Inspection. Every bail agent or permittee shall keep complete records of all business done under authority of his license or under the authority of the license of any bail solicitor, bail agent or bail permittee employed by him. All records kept by such agent or permittee, including all documents and copies thereof shall be open to inspection or examination by the commissioner or his representatives at all reasonable times, at the principal place of business of the licensee as designated in his license. Such records shall include at least the following information as to each bail transaction shown either in one of the forms required by the provisions of these rules or in a separate book, ledger, or card record:

(a) The full name and address of the arrestee.

(b) The date of arrest, the offense with which the arrestee was charged, the penal amount of the bail, the premium for the undertaking of bail or the amount charged for the bail bond, the date the bail was filed or delivered, and the court or public official before whom the arrestee must appear.

(c) The full name and address of the person furnishing information leading to the solicitation or negotiation of the bail, the date and time such information was received, the manner in which it was received, the connection or relationship to the arrestee of the person other than the arrestee furnishing such information, and the name of the person receiving such information.

(d) If the bail was negotiated with any person other than the arrestee, the full name, address and connection or relationship to the arrestee of such person, and the name of the person who carried out the negotiations on behalf of the licensee.

(e) If the bail was negotiated directly with the arrestee, a full statement of the manner in which the arrestee communicated with the licensee and the name of the person receiving such communication.

(f) The full name and address of each and every person directly or indirectly paying, promising to pay, or guaranteeing the payment of, the whole or any part of the premium, guard fees, charges for extraordinary services, or collateral made or deposited in connection with a bail transaction.

(g) The name of any bail licensee from whom the business was accepted or to whom commission was promised or paid in connection therewith, and the amount of commission promised or paid.

(h) The name of any person who received or was promised any portion of a premium, guard fee, charge or commission or was compensated in any manner directly or indirectly on account of any bail transaction.

(i) If any valuable consideration other that money was received in connection with a bail transaction, a full statement in explanation of such consideration and the circumstances attendant thereto.

(j) Where a writ bond was issued, the name of the attorney appearing thereon.

(k) A separate book record which shall show the date of receipt of any collateral as a guarantee in a bail transaction, the name of the person from whom it was received, the name of the person receiving it, a complete description of the collateral, the amount of bail guaranteed, the amount of premium guaranteed and the disposition of the collateral. If the collateral was returned, the date of its return and the name of the person to whom it was returned.

2101. Co-partnership Records; Filings. During the period when two or more bail licensees are conducting their business as a partnership pursuant to Section 2061, such licensees may combine their books and records and make a joint filing with the commissioner of all forms used by them as a partnership, provided, however, that such books and records shall identify the member of the partnership who actually transacted each individual bail transaction or portion thereof.

2101.1. Records; Licensed Employees. Every employing bail agent or permittee shall keep at his office all books and records concerning the bail transactions of himself and his employees while acting as such, and such employees may use all forms filed, directly or by reference, with the commissioner by such employer; provided, however, that such books and records shall identify the particular person who actually transacted each individual bail transaction or portion thereof. But the employed bail agent or permittee is responsible or the maintenance of such records, and the proper use of such forms for the transactions in which he participates.

2101.2. Records; Temporary Associations. If two or more bail agents or permittees are temporarily associated for the purposes of a single or series of bail transactions, each shall be responsible for keeping sufficient records to identify the transactions and to meet the requirements of this article with respect to the portion of the transaction conducted by him.

2101.3. Records; Temporarily Conducting Business. During the time a bail agent or permittee is temporarily conducting the business of another bail agent or permittee as provided in Section 2065(e), such bail agent or permittee shall be responsible for the proper entries in and the retention of the books and records of such other bail agent or permittee but he may use the forms and documents usually used by the permanent owner of the bail business. Following such temporary conduct of his business the permanent owner of such business is responsible for the retention of such books and records.

2102. Use of Filed Documents and Forms. Except as provided in Sections 2101.1 and 2101.3, inclusive, every bail agent and permittee shall use the forms and documents filed, directly or by reference, by him with the commissioner as an individual and shall be individually responsible for the proper entries in and the retention of all books and records.

2103. Information; Not Required; Severability. Any bail licensee may secure from any person with whom he engaged in a bail transaction information in addition to that required by these rules or his signature to documents other than those required by these rules. If such information is secured as a part of the same document which contains any of the information required by these rules, it shall be clearly severable and the licensee, in using such document, may, at his discretion, omit the use of the portion of it which is not required by these rules.

2104. Destruction of Records. Five years after the final completion of all parts of a bail transaction, a bail licensee may destroy his records pertaining to such transactions.

CHAPTER 8:
BAIL BONDS - TODAY AND TOMORROW

The bail bond business will be around for a long time to come, that is, if you keep up with the crime index in the U.S. Today's bail bondsmen are faced with basically the same crimes as those ten years ago except for crack cocaine. The crack epidemic in the early 80's up until the mid 90's made quite a few bail bondsmen wealthy. Because along with the crack came a surge in auto thefts, burglaries, prostitution, robberies and even murder.

One area of crime that has shown a drastic increase is drug possession, trafficking and manufacturing. The fact that many counterfeit and addictive drugs are easy to make in a garage or in the back room of a trailer, using items available from a drugstore, make abuse even more rampart as well as uncontrollable.

With city, state and federal budget cutbacks, and the fact that criminals outnumber the police force, adds a buffer of insurance for the bail bondsman of today and tomorrow.

THE FUTURE

The future of the bail bonds business looks bright in terms of crime. In 1995 alone, there were over 14 million arrest made in the U. S. Just think, out of those many people arrested, all a bondsman needed to do was bail out a small percentage of this group to make a decent living.

Larceny-theft, drug abuse violations and driving under the influence accounted for a large majority of arrests. Also in this same category, drunkness, disorderly conduct and liquor laws placed many citizens in jail.

A startling statistic regarding the crime index in the U. S. reports that the under-25 age group was responsible for over 45 percent of violent crime arrest and over 55 percent of property crime arrests. As mentioned throughout this book "as long as teenagers are growing up to become adults, crime in America is here to stay".

Another encouraging report on crime showed a 5 percent rise in the number of male arrests from 1993 to 1994, and a 7 percent boost in female arrest for that same period.

Maybe one day we can live in a crime-free society, but until that day comes... crime pays... especially if you're in the bail bond business.

EPILOGUE

Anybody can write a bond - and that's a fact. The name of the game in this business is being able to recover and being able to sleep at night. If you have just posted a bond for $20,000.00 and did not check out the collateral fully and come to find out that you overlooked something crucial that could cost you... you are in for some sleepless nights. You will be awake wishing and praying that this particular case is exonerated fast without any complications such as a bail forfeiture.

There is no explanation how it feels to pay off $20,000.00 cash, on a bond without any means of recovery. You're looking at $20,000.00 down the drain, money that you will never see again. And this is exactly what happens when you cannot recover from a bail skip - you throw money down the drain.

The purpose of this book is to prepare you in making a profitable living in this business... and if you do decide to become a professional bondsman, remember that anybody can write a bond. It's the staying in business, and not paying off more than you write that wins. so write good bonds, take in real good collateral, screen your clients and you will rank among the professionals in this business that walk away with some of the rewards that this business has to offer.

CHAPTER 9:
FORMS USED IN THE BUSINESS

This chapter deals with tools of the trade... the various forms used in the bail bond business. In this section, the intent is to familiarize you with some of the forms you will come in contact with as a bail bondsman. There are other forms used in the business, but these represent the most common ones you should become familiar with.

INITIAL STOCK

All of the forms and documents to be used in your business operations will be supplied to you by your surety insurance company via the general agent that represents the surety that you will be writing for. As each insurance company supplies it's agents with their own standard forms and documents, these sample forms illustrated on the next pages are only to familiarize you with the different documents that are used in the business. (Some of the forms have been reduced for convenience.) You will also see how the forms should be properly filled out.

THE APPLICATION FOR BAIL

The application is filled out by you as you the screen the indemnitor(s) as well as the defendant (when he/she is released). Every question should be answered. By filling out each application completely, you get to know who you are dealing with. And if the time comes when there is a bail forfeiture, you will have something to go on.

APPLICATION FOR BAIL

P.A. # ____ Amt. ____ Exec. Date ____ Arr. Date ____

BOOKING INFORMATION

Booking Name ____ A.K.A. ____
Booking # ____ Where Held ____ Arr. By ____ F.B.I. # ____ C.I.I. # ____
Charges ____ Case # ____ Date to Appear ____ Time ____
Court ____ Jud. Dist. ____ At ____ County ____
Where Arrested ____ Co-Defendants ____

INFORMATION ON DEFENDANT

St. Add. ____ City ____ Phone ____ How Long ____
Former Add. ____ How Long ____
Years in City ____ County ____ State ____ Last County ____ Last State ____
Employed By ____ Occupation ____ Phone ____ How Long ____
Employer's Add. ____ Superior ____ Shift ____
Previous Employment ____ Address ____ When ____
D.O.B. ____ Sex ____ Height ____ Weight ____ Hair ____ Eyes ____ S.S. # ____ D.L. # ____
I.D. Marks ____ Race ____ Moustache ____ Glasses ____ Where Born ____
Previous Arrest Charge ____ Court ____ County ____ When ____
Disposition ____ Previous Bail ____ With Whom ____ Amount ____ Case Pending? ____
On Probation? ____ Where ____ Probation Officer ____
Vehicle - Make ____ Model ____ Year ____ Color ____ License # ____
Military Branch ____ Serial # ____ Discharge Date ____ Union ____ Local # ____
Date ____ SIGNATURE OF DEFENDANT ____

INFORMATION ON DEFENDANT'S FAMILY

Spouse ____ Address ____ Phone ____ How Long ____
Employed By ____ Address ____ Phone ____ How Long ____
Married - When ____ Where ____ Spouse's Maiden Name ____ D.O.B. ____
Previous Spouse ____ Address ____ City ____ Phone ____
Children - Name & Age ____
Mother ____ Address ____ Phone ____
Father ____ Address ____ Phone ____
Spouse's Mother ____ Address ____ Phone ____
Spouse's Father ____ Address ____ Phone ____
Defendant's Brother ____ Address ____ Phone ____
Defendant's Sister ____ Address ____ Phone ____
Best Friend ____ Address ____ Phone ____
Defendant's Attorney ____ City ____ Phone ____
Date ____ SIGNATURE OF DEFENDANT ____

INFORMATION ON INDEMNITOR

Indemnitor's Name ____ Address ____ Phone ____
Social Security # ____ D.L. # ____ D.O.B. ____ Rel. to Def. ____
Employed By ____ Address ____ Phone ____
Occupation ____ How Long ____ Superior ____ Monthly Income ____
Bank ____ Branch ____ Account # ____ Type ____ Balance ____
Spouse ____ Address ____ Phone ____
Employed By ____ Address ____ Phone ____
Vehicle - Make ____ Model ____ Year ____ Color ____ License ____
Registered Owner ____ Legal Owner ____ Liens ____
Real Property ____ In Who's Name ____ How Long ____
Lot ____ Block ____ Tract ____ Maps In Book ____ Page ____
Value ____ Equity ____ Financed By ____
Notations ____

I certify that the above information is true and correct. ____ DATE ____ SIGNATURE OF INDEMNITOR

STATEMENT OF INFORMATION REQUIRED BY SECTION 2100, CALIFORNIA ADMINISTRATION CODE

Full name of person supplying information	Name of person negotiating bail	Name of person receiving information
Address	Address	Date and time information received
Connection or relationship to defendant	Connection or relationship to defendant	Manner in which information received
If same was defendant, how did he communicate?	Name of licensee who negotiated transaction	Name of other agent involved and commission pa

If writ ____ Name of Attorney ____ Name and sum paid unlicensed persons and service performed

Was consideration other than money received? YES ☐ NO ☐ If yes, explain in detail and attach statement.

THE BAIL AGREEMENT

Everyone who negotiates bail through your office should receive a copy of the bail agreement. This document will inform the indemnitor of their obligations to you and your insurance company. Make sure that it is dated and signed properly by the indemnitor(s).

BAIL AGREEMENT

The undersigned, called "First Party," make(s) application to ______________________ called "Second Party," for execution by ABC SURETY CO a corporation, called "Surety," of a Bail Undertaking herein referred to as "Bail Bond" in the penal amount of $ ______________________ for ______________________ called "Principal"; and in consideration of Second Party arranging for execution of or continuance of this Bail Bond, First Party does jointly and severally agree as follows:

FIRST: To pay Second Party $ ______________ per annum for this Bail Bond. The premium is fully earned upon the release of Principal. The fact that Defendant may have been improperly arrested, or his bail reduced or his case dismissed, shall not obligate the return of any portion of said premium. This Bond is renewable each year. First Party agrees to pay to Second Party a renewal premium in the amount stated above, twelve months after the date on which this Bond was executed. If said renewal premium is not paid upon written demand therefor, Second Party or Surety has the right to surrender Principal, as provided in the California Penal Code, Section 1300, and exonerate the Bond.

SECOND: To reimburse Second Party and Surety for actual expenses incurred by Second Party or Surety in connection with the arranging and/or execution of Bail Bond or any renewal or substitution thereof whether or not said Principal refuses to be released after arrangements have been initiated by Second Party, in accordance with the regulations of the Insurance Commissioner in effect at the time such expenses are incurred.

THIRD: To reimburse Second Party and Surety for actual expenses incurred and caused by a breach by the Principal of any of the terms for which the application and Bail Bond were written not in excess of the penal amount of the Bail Bond including all expenses or liabilities incurred as a result of searching for, recapturing or returning Principal to custody, incurred by Second Party or Surety or as necessary in apprehending or endeavoring to apprehend Principal, including legal fees incurred by Second Party or Surety in making application to a court for an order to vacate or to set aside the order of forfeiture or Summary Judgment entered thereon. However, no expenses or liabilities incurred for recapturing or returning Principal to custody shall be chargeable after the entry of Summary Judgment.

FOURTH: To pay the Second Party or the Surety, in the event that it is necessary for them to institute suit for a breach of this agreement, a reasonable attorney's fee which shall, in no event, be less than the sum of twenty-five dollars ($25.00).

FIFTH: To pay Second Party or Surety as collateral upon demand, the penal amount of Bail Bond whenever Second Party or Surety, as a result of information concealed or misrepresented by the First Party or Principal or other reasonable cause, any one of which was material to hazard assumed, deems payment necessary to protect the Second Party or Surety hereunder. Where, as a result of judicial action, bail has been increased, and no collateral or insufficient collateral in the sole discretion of Second Party or Surety, is furnished to indemnify against such increase in the bail, Second Party or Surety may demand such collateral as will indemnify them against such increased bail.

SIXTH: To pay Second Party or Surety immediately upon demand after entry of Summary Judgment, pursuant to California Penal Code, Section 1306.

SEVENTH: To aid Second Party or Surety in securing release or exoneration of Second Party or Surety from all liability under Bail Bond, including the surrender of Principal to Court should Second Party or Surety deem such action advisable.

EIGHTH: That all money or other property which the First Party has deposited or may deposit with the Second Party or the Surety may be applied as collateral security or indemnity for matters contained herein, and to accomplish the purposes contained herein, the Second Party and/or the Surety is authorized to lawfully levy upon said collateral in the manner provided by law and to apply the proceeds therefrom and any and all money deposited to payment of or reimbursement for the hereinabove liabilities, losses, costs, damages and expenses. If collateral received by Second Party is in excess of the bail forfeited, such excess shall be returned to the depositor immediately upon the application of the collateral to the forfeiture, subject to any claim of Second Party and Surety for unpaid premium or the hereinabove charges.

NINTH: Second Party or Surety shall not surrender Principal to custody prior to the time specified in the Bail Bond for the appearance of the Principal, or prior to any other occasion when the presence of the Principal in court is lawfully required, without returning all premium paid therefor, unless as a result of judicial action, information concealed or misrepresented by the Principal, or other reasonable cause, any one of which was material to the hazard assumed, the hazard was substantially increased and the additional premium, if any, for such increased hazard was not paid within a reasonable time.

TENTH: The obligations hereunder are joint and several and any amounts due shall bear interest at the maximum rate of interest allowed by law. The Second Party and the Surety shall not be first obliged to proceed against the Principal on Bail Bond before having recourse against the First Party or any one of them, the First Party hereby expressly waiving the benefit of law requiring the Second Party or the Surety to make claim upon or to proceed or enforce its remedies against the Principal before making demand upon or proceeding and/or enforcing its remedies against any one or more of the First Party.

ELEVENTH: In making application for Bail Bond, each of us warrants all statements made on this application and financial statement to be true, and we agree to advise Second Party or Surety of any change, including but not limited to change of address or employment of either the Principal or of any of the First Party, or any other material change in circumstances within forty-eight (48) hours after knowledge such change shall have occurred.

TWELFTH: The undersigned agree that these obligations apply to all other Bail Bonds executed for the same charge for which the above mentioned Bail Bond was executed, or any charge arising out of the same transaction, regardless of whether said Bail Bonds are filed before or after conviction, but not in a greater amount.

IN WITNESS WHEREOF, the First Party whose names are subscribed to the Bail Agreement executed herewith each represents: I have read the Bail Agreement and I know the contents thereof; that I hereby acknowledge receipt of a copy of said Bail Agreement; that I am the true and lawful owner of the property, whether real or personal, which is set forth in the Application for Bail (which Application is made a part hereof by reference as though herein fully set forth) as being my property and that I own such property free and clear of all liens or encumbrances except as so noted, and I further promise not to transfer or encumber any of said property until my liability on said Bail Agreement has been released. I understand the Second Party and/or Surety is permitting the said bail to remain in force upon reliance of the statements made by me and do now set their hand this __________ day of ______________________, 19______________.

Defendant
SIGNATURE ______________________

NAME ______________ Address ______________ City ______________ Zip ______________

Phone ______________ Drivers Lic. ______________ S.S. No. ______________ Date of Birth ______________

Indemnitor
SIGNATURE ______________________

NAME ______________ Address ______________ City ______________ Zip ______________

Phone ______________ Drivers Lic. ______________ S.S. No. ______________ Date of Birth ______________

Indemnitor
SIGNATURE ______________________

NAME ______________ Address ______________ City ______________ Zip ______________

Phone ______________ Drivers Lic. ______________ S.S. No. ______________ Date of Birth ______________

Indemnitor
SIGNATURE ______________________

NAME ______________ Address ______________ City ______________ Zip ______________

Phone ______________ Drivers Lic. ______________ S.S. No. ______________ Date of Birth ______________

Indemnitor
SIGNATURE ______________________

NAME ______________ Address ______________ City ______________ Zip ______________

Phone ______________ Drivers Lic. ______________ S.S. No. ______________ Date of Birth ______________

RECEIVED COPY OF BAIL BOND AGREEMENT

THE BAIL INFORMATION SHEET

When you contact the jail in order to bail someone out, the jailer will supply you with the information necessary to write the bond. Items 1 thru 7 are basically what will be needed to write a bond. Always ask for a physical description of the defendant, because in the event of a bail forfeiture, you will at least have a basic description.

BAIL INFORMATION SHEET

(1) Booking Name______________________________

(2) Booking Number______________________________

(3) Case Number______________________________

(4) Charge(s)______________________________

(5) Bail Amount______________________________

(6) Court______________________________

(7) Date________________ Time________________

Jail______________________________

Date of Birth______________ Date of Arrest__________

Age________________ Race________________

Height________________ Sex________________

Weight__________ Eyes__________ Hair__________

Alias______________________________

Indemnitor(s)______________________________

Telephone Number______________________________

THE FACE SHEET

The information from your bail information sheet that you get from the jailer will be used to write the face sheet and the power of attorney. The face sheet is attached to the power of attorney (see next page). These two documents together are called the bond. This is what you present to the jail in order to have a defendant released.

ABC SURETY INSURANCE COMPANY

YOUR BAIL BOND AGENCY
1154 HOWARD ST.
LOS ANGELES, CA. 90292
I. D. NO. 5226
(213) 555-1212

(PLACE BAIL AGENT'S ADDRESS STAMP HERE)

BAIL BOND

NO. Power of Attorney No. (see next page)
(POWER OF ATTORNEY WITH THIS NUMBER MUST BE ATTACHED.)

IN THE (6) Municipal / Superior COURT OF THE (6) City or District JUDICIAL DISTRICT

COUNTY OF (6) Los Angeles (example), STATE OF CALIFORNIA.

THE PEOPLE OF THE STATE OF CALIFORNIA, Plaintiff,

vs.

(1)
Defendant.

CASE NO. (3)
DIV. NO. (6) optional

Defendant (1) (NAME OF DEFENDANT) (2) (BOOKING NO.)

having been admitted to bail in the sum of (5)

Dollars ($ (5)) and ordered to appear in the above-entitled court

on (7) (DATE OF APPEARANCE) 19___, on (4) (STATE "MISDEMEANOR" OR "FELONY") charge/s;

Now, the ABC SURETY INSURANCE CO., a Corporation, hereby undertakes that the above-named defendant will appear in the above-named court on the date above set forth to answer any change in any accusatory pleading based upon the acts supporting the complaint filed against him/her and as duly authorized amendments thereof, in whatever court it may be prosecuted, and will at all times hold him/herself amendable to the orders and process of the court, and if convicted, will appear for pronouncement of judgment or grant of probation; or if he/she fails to perform either of these conditions, that the ABC SURETY INSURANCE CO., a Corporation, will pay to the people of the State of California, the sum of (5) dollars ($ (5)).

If the forfeiture of this bond be ordered by the Court, judgment may be summarily made and entered forthwith against the said ABC SURETY INSURANCE CO. a Corporation, for the amount of its undertaking herein as provided by Sections 1305 and 1306 of the Penal Code.

THIS BOND IS VOID IF WRITTEN FOR AN AMOUNT GREATER THAN THE POWER OF ATTORNEY ATTACHED HERETO, IF MORE THAN ONE SUCH POWER IS ATTACHED, OR IF WRITTEN AFTER THE EXPIRATION DATE IF SPECIFIED ON THE ATTACHED POWER OF ATTORNEY.

By (Signed by agent appointed by insurance company)
ATTORNEY-IN-FACT

I certify under penalty of perjury that I am a licensed bail agent of the and that I am executing this bond on (Date bond posted) (DATE)

at (City and State where bond written) (LOCATION)

(Agent that writes the bond)
(SIGNATURE OF LICENSED AGENT)

THE PREMIUM CHARGED FOR THIS BOND PER ANNUM IS: $ (Usually 10% of bail amount)

Approved this _____ day of _____, 19___
_____ (TITLE)

***NOTE:** This is an Appearance Bond and cannot be construed as a guarantee for failure to provide payments, back alimony payments, FINES, or Wage Law claims, nor can it be used as a Bond on Appeal.*

POWER OF ATTORNEY

The power of attorney along with the face sheet is what you present to the jail or court for the release of a defendant. This is called the bond. This is what obligates you and your insurance company to see to it that the defendant makes all court appearances until the bond is exonerated.

COURT COPY

POWER OF ATTORNEY

ABC SURETY INSURANCE COMPANY

OF CALIFORNIA

POWER AMOUNT $ 5,000 POWER NO. 044146

KNOW ALL MEN BY THESE PRESENTS that the ABC SURETY Co. of CA. corporation duly organized and existing under the laws of the State of CA., and by the authority of the Resolution adopted by the Board of Directors at a meeting duly called and held on March 21, 1984 which said Resolution has not been amended or rescinded, does constitute and appoint and by these presents does make, constitute and appoint the named agent its true and lawful Attorney-in-Fact for it and in its name, place and stead, to execute, seal and deliver for and on its behalf and as its act and deed, as surety, a bail bond only, Authority of such Attorney-in-Fact is limited to appearance bonds and cannot be construed to guarantee for failure to provide payments, back alimony payments, fines or wage law claims, on behalf of below named defendant.

This power void if altered or erased, void if used with other powers of this company, void if used to furnish bail in excess of the stated face amount of this power, and can only be used once. The obligation of the company shall not exceed the sum of $5,000 and provided this Power-of-Attorney is filed with the bond and retained as a part of the court records. The said Attorney-in-Fact is hereby authorized to insert in this Power-of-Attorney the name of the person on whose behalf this bond was given.

IN WITNESS WHEREOF, ABC SURETY INS. CO. OF CA. has caused these presents to be signed by its duly authorized attorney in fact, proper for the purpose and its corporate seal to be hereunto affixed this 11 day of September 1985

Bond Amount $ 5,000.00

Defendant Anthony Tyrone.

Court Div. 130 Municipal

City Los Angeles

State California

If rewrite, original # ______

Executing Agent (Your Name)

By ______

Attorney-in-Fact

APPEAL BOND

What differentiates the Appeal Bond from the Standard bail bond can be seen in the top left corner of the form. Also you can see that there is a little more information required on the Appeal Bond regarding the judge's name and court.

A B C
INSURANCE
COMPANY

Your Bail Bond Agency
1154 Rich Blvd.
LOS ANGELES, CA 90210
(310) 555-1212
I. D. No. 2226

(PLACE BAIL AGENT'S ADDRESS STAMP HERE)

APPEAL BAIL BOND NO. RW-26526
(POWER OF ATTORNEY WITH THIS NUMBER MUST BE ATTACHED.)

NORWALK SUPERIOR COURT OF THE STATE OF CALIFORNIA FOR THE COUNTY OF LOS ANGELES

THE PEOPLE OF THE STATE OF CALIFORNIA, Plaintiff, CASE NO. A 141144

vs.

BETTY JONES
Defendant.

An order having been duly made on the 2ND day of JUNE, 19 96, by the Hon CLARENCE A. MACKIN a Judge of the NORWALK SUPERIOR Court of the DOWNEY JUDICIAL DISTRICT County of LOS ANGELES, State of California, that said Defendant BETTY JONES be admitted to bail in the sum of TWENTY FIVE THOUSAND & xx/00 Dollars ($25,000.00) pending the hearing and determination of the appeal of the defendant from the judgment and sentence heretofore rendered in the above entitled cause, in the above entitled court on the 1ST day of JULY, 19 96, wherein said defendant was charged with and convicted of the crime of "FELONY" 11351 H.&S

and said defendant having duly appealed for said conviction and judgment herein, and said defendant having been duly admitted to bail pending the hearing and determination of said appeal in the sum of TWENTY FIVE THOUSAND Dollars ($25,000.00)

NOW, THEREFORE, We the hereby undertake that the above named Defendant BETTY JONES will surrender himself in execution of the judgment, upon its being affirmed or modified, or upon the appeal being dismissed, or that, in case the judgment be reversed and that the cause be remanded for a new trial, that he will appear in the court to which said cause may be remanded, and submit himself to the orders and process thereof; and that if he fails to perform either of these conditions that we will pay to the People of the State of California the sum of TWENTY FIVE THOUSAND Dollars ($25,000.00) in lawful money of the United States. If the forfeiture of this bond be ordered by the Court, judgment may be summarily made and entered forthwith against the said for the amount of its undertaking herein as provided by Sections 1305 and 1306 of the Penal Code.

THIS BOND IS VOID IF WRITTEN FOR AN AMOUNT GREATER THAN THE POWER OF ATTORNEY ATTACHED HERETO, IF MORE THAN ONE SUCH POWER IS ATTACHED, OR IF WRITTEN AFTER THE EXPIRATION DATE IF SPECIFIED ON THE ATTACHED POWER OF ATTORNEY.

CORPORATE SEAL

By John Q Bail Bondsman (SEAL)
ATTORNEY-IN-FACT

I certify under penalty of perjury that I am a licensed bail agent of the and that I am executing this bond on 6-2-96 at LOS ANGELES, CALIFORNIA
(LOCATION)

John Q Bail Bondsman
(SIGNATURE OF LICENSED AGENT)

THE PREMIUM CHARGED FOR THIS BOND PER ANNUM IS: $ 2,500.00

Approved this ______ day of ______, 19____
(TITLE)

NOTE: This is an Appearance Bond and cannot be construed as a guarantee for failure to provide payments, back alimony payments, FINES, or Wage Law claims.

BAIL AGENT'S REPORT

This report is an account of the bonds that were written by your bail bond agency. Your general agent will instruct you on completing this report and also inform you on how often this report is to be mailed in to the insurance company that you will be writing for. The sample entry shows only one transaction, although you will have many such entries once you get started.

AGENT'S BAIL REPORT

REPORT NO. ____________
DATE ____________
AGENT ____________
ACCOUNT NO. ____________

[illegible]	2 EFFECTIVE [illegible]	3 DEFENDANT	4 LIABILITY AMOUNT	5 GROSS	6 NET. PREM. DUE COMPANY	7 B.U.F. RESERVE DUE COMPANY
044146	9-11-85	Anthony Tyrone	$5,000.00	$500.00	$80.00	$100.00
		Note: Sample shows -				
		1. Bond Number				
		2. Date Bond Written				
		3. Defendant's Name				
		4. Bond Amount				
		5. Amount Charged (10%)				
		6. Amount To Ins. Co.				
		7. Amount to Build Up Fund				
		TOTAL				

EXONERATION and DISCHARGES

POWER NO.	DATE POWER ISSUE	DEFENDANT	LIABILITY AMOUNT	DATE DISC./EXON

LIABILITY SUMMARY	
OUTSTANDING LAST REPORT	
WRITTEN THIS REPORT	
TOTAL	
DISC./EXON. THIS REPORT	
OUTSTANDING LIABILITY	
B U F RESERVE SUMMARY	
BALANCE LAST REPORT	
DEPOSIT THIS REPORT	
TOTAL	

MOTION TO EXONERATE BOND

The motion to exonerate bond is used when a defendant has missed a court appearance or jumped bail, resulting in a bail forfeiture. This motion is presented to the court when the defendant is found and brought back to justice. The bonding company is relieved of any liability, once approved by the court.

IN THE SUPERIOR COURT OF THE LOS ANGELES DISTRICT,
COUNTY OF LOS ANGELES, STATE OF CALIFORNIA

PEOPLE OF THE STATE OF CALIFORNIA, Plaintiff, vs. BOB LEE Defendant,	CASE NO. A524344 DECLARATION OF BAIL AGENT IN SUPPORT OF MOTION

John Q. Bail Bondsman declares as follows, That he is the Bail Agent in the above action. That said bail was ordered forfeited on 2-26-96, mailed 3-1-96.

That the defendant, BOB LEE appeared in court on this case after the date of forfeiture and was sentences on this case. Therefore, under Section 1305 of the Penal Code, I respectfully request that this bail be exonerated. Thank You.

WHEREFORE, declarant prays that the order forfeiting the bail be vacated and the said bond exonerated.

I certify and declare under penalty of perjury that the foregoing is true and correct of my own personal knowledge, except as to those matters alleged to be based on information and belief, and as to them, I in good faith believe them to be true.

Executed at Los Angeles, California on May 23, 19 96.
City and State

John Q. Bail Bondsman
DECLARANT.

MOTION TO HAVE TIME TOLLED

The motion to have time tolled on a bond is a strategy used to buy additional time in locating a defendant on a bail forfeiture. Usually the bonding company knows the whereabouts of a defendant and is pleading with the court for more time in order to bring in the defendant.

IN THE SUPERIOR COURT OF THE LOS ANGELES JUDICIAL DISTRICT,

COUNTY OF LOS ANGELES STATE OF CALIFORNIA

PEOPLE OF THE STATE OF CALIFORNIA, Plaintiff	DECLARATION OF BAIL AGENT
vs.	Case Number A751599
RAY SCOTT, Defendant	

I John Q. Bail Bondsman, being first duly sworn, deposes and says:

That he is the bail agent in the above entitled action, whose bail was forfeited on 12-24-95 by reason of the defendant's failure to appear on that date.

That I would appreciate very much if the court would consider tolling the time on this case on defendant Ray Scott because this agency via information from a XYZ Investigators, Inc. The investigation revealed to our agency places the defendant's whereabouts in Miami, Florida. If the Court would please grant a month on this case, I think that the defendant can be brought back before this Court, and possibly as soon as possible. Thank You.

That the defendant's failure to appear as aforesaid was without the knowledge or consent of the bail.

WHEREFORE, affiant prays that the order toll time on bond.

I certify and declare under penalty of perjury that the foregoing is true and correct.

Executed at Los Angeles, California June 2, 1996

By John Q. Bail Bondsman
Bail Agent

GLOSSARY

APPEAL BOND	When a defendant has been found guilty of a crime, and he/she faces jail; or has been sentenced to prison, the defendant, under certain conditions and circumstances, can appeal the conviction and be retried in a court of law. In order to remain out of jail until the case is retried, an appeal bond is posted.
ARRESTEE	Any person actually detained or subject to detention in custody whose release may lawfully be effected by bail; one that is under arrest; used in the same context as defendant in bail proceedings.
BAIL	Security given for the due appearance of a prisoner in order to obtain his/her release from imprisonment; To deliver (property) in trust to another for a special purpose and for a limited period.
BAIL FORFEITURE	An occurrence whereas a defendant fails to appear in court on a given date.
BAIL INFORMATION	This information is supplied to you from the jailer when negotiating bail. You will use this information to write a bond.
BAIL SKIP	Person or persons who fail to appear in court when scheduled.
BOND EXONERATION	The judicial process by which the bonding company is relieved of all obligations and responsibilities associated with a bond posted in behalf of a defendant.
BOUNTY HUNTER	One that tracks down and captures outlaws and criminals for a fee.

BUILD-UP FUND An account set up by an insurance company for bondsmen, to serve as a means of protecting the surety against losing money on a bail forfeiture; Also known as a reserve account for the bondsman.

COLLATERAL Property pledged; (1) as security, additional to ones personal obligation; (2) by an indemnitor to protect the interest of the bondsman should a bail forfeiture occur.

CUSTODY To be in jail, incarcerated. To have custody of a prisoner, a State must hold that person in one of its facilities.

DEFENDANT A person required to make answer in a legal action; A person against whom an action is brought. In the bail bond business, this term refers to the person that you bail out of jail who is to stand trial and prove his/her innocence. Also used in the same context as arrestee.

DETENTION STATUS This term distinguishes between prisoners, usually in jail, who were convicted or who are awaiting judgement.

DOCKET SHEET A chronological history of a defendant, usually filed at the courthouse. It contains the status of a criminal case, the defendant's booking name, bond number, case number, court appearances, etc.

IN CUSTODY Meaning the same as "in jail".

INDEMNITOR One who compensates for loss of damage sustained; One who gives security against future loss. From the bail bond business point of view, the indemnitor is the one who puts up collateral and is responsible for paying off a bond in the event of a bail forfeiture.

JAILER A peace officer who is responsible for giving bail information to the bondsman regarding a defendant in custody.

JURISDICTION — Refers to a unit of government or to the legal authority to exercise governmental power. Meaning, prisoners under a State's jurisdiction may be in the custody of local jails.

MATERIAL WITNESS BOND — A legal device for witnesses, to insure that they appear in court.

MOTION — As used in the bail bond business, a legal document filed by a bonding company to have a bond exonerated or have the time tolled on a bond.

NO BAIL HOLD — A term used when a defendant is not eligible for bail. Usually set for parole violators or high risk criminals

OFFENSE — An infraction of the law, i.e., felony, misdemeanor, federal.

POSTING FEE — Travel expenses incurred by agent in the process of posting a bond; Usually for posting bail in a county other than where bail was arranged; Often included when making house calls.

O.R. — The judicial process whereby a defendant is released on his own recognizance; Meaning that the defendant promises to appear in court on a given date and time, and his/her failure to do so will result in the issuance of an warrant for his/her arrest. No bail is required on this type of release.

PREMIUM — Fee charged by bail bondsmen in order to post bond for the release of a defendant in custody, usually 10% of the bail amount.

RECOVER — The means by which you recoup from a loss; To obtain again after losing.

STAKE OUT — A surveillance maintained by an agency (police, bounty hunter, etc.) of an area for a person suspected of criminal activity, or a fugitive from justice.

STRAIGHT PICKUP When a bounty hunter is hired to bring a defendant in on a bail forfeiture, whereas the defendant's whereabouts are known and the defendant is complications.

SURRENDER The delivery of a principal into lawful custody by his bail, also called surrender by bail; the delivery of a fugitive from justice by one agency to another.

TRAFFIC WARRANT Moving violations governed by the Vehicle Code where the defendant has failed to satisfy judgement and an arrest warrant is issued for defendant's arrest

WATCH COMMANDER A peace officer at a jail who is in charge of prisoners. If a bondsman has a problem obtaining bail information or posting a bond at a jail facility, the watch commander is the person to contact.

APPENDIXES

FORFEITURE TIME

The forfeiture time is the maximum time given by the court for a defendant to be brought back into court when the defendant fails to appear. If the defendant does not appear or is surrendered to the court in the allotted time, the full amount of the bond posted is due and payable to the court. Some states have what's called remittance time. This is the length of time after a bail forfeiture has been paid off, that the court will refund all or part of the bond amount if the defendant is surrendered or found in custody.

STATE	FORFEITURE TIME
Alabama	Court Discretion
Alaska	120 Days
Arizona	None
Arkansas	Court Discretion
California	180 Days
Colorado	30 to 90 Days
Connecticut	30 Days
Delaware	30 Days
Florida	30 Days
Georgia	30 to 90 Days
Hawaii	10 Days
Idaho	21 Days
Illinois	30 Days
Indiana	180 Days
Iowa	10 Days
Kansas	6 Weeks
Kentucky	None
Louisiana	180 Days

STATE	FORFEITURE TIME
Maryland	90 Days
Massachusetts	Court Discretion
Michigan	30 Days
Minnesota	None
Mississippi	180 Days
Missouri	None
Montana	30 Days
Nebraska	90 Days
Nevada	90 Days
New Hampshire	Court Discretion
New Jersey	Court Discretion
New Mexico	14 Days
New York	30 to 60 Days
North Carolina	30 Days
North Dakota	Court Discretion
Ohio	30 to 90 Days
Oklahoma	30 Days
Oregon	30 Days
Pennsylvania	30 Days
Rhode Island	Court Discretion
South Carolina	Court Discretion
South Dakota	Court Discretion
Tennessee	15 Days
Texas	20 Days
Utah	14 Days
Vermont	20 Days
Washington	60 Days
West Virginia	10 Days

STATE	FORFEITURE TIME
Wisconsin	60 Days
Wyoming	30 Days

STATE INSURANCE COMMISSIONERS

STATE	NAME AND TITLE	ADDRESS
ALABAMA	THARPE FORRESTER COMMISSIONER OF INSURANCE	64 NORTH UNION ST. MONTGOMERY 36130
ALASKA	KENNETH MOORE DIRECTOR OF INSURANCE	POUCH "D" JUNEAU 99811
ARIZONA	J. MICHAEL LOW DIRECTOR OF INSURANCE	1601 WEST JEFFERSON PHOENIX 85007
ARKANSAS	WILLIAM H.L. WOODYARD III INSURANCE COMMISSIONER LITTLE ROCK 72204	400-18 UNIVERSITY TOWER BLVD.
CALIFORNIA	WESLEY J. KINDER INSURANCE COMMISSIONER LOS ANGELES 90005	3450 WILSHIRE BLVD. ROOM 201
COLORADO	J. RICHARD BARNES COMMISSIONER OF INSURANCE	106 STATE OFFICE BLVD. DENVER 80203
CONNECTICUT	JOSEPH C. MIKE INSURANCE COMMISSIONER HARTFORD 06115	165 CAPITOL AVENUE. ROOM 425
DELAWARE	DAVID H. ELLIOTT INSURANCE COMMISSIONER	21 THE GREEN DOVER 19901
D.C.	JAMES R. MONTGOMERY III SUPERINTENDENT OF INS.	614 "H" STREET N.W. ROOM 512 WASHINGTON 20001
FLORIDA	WILLIAM D. GUNTER INSURANCE COMMISSIONER	STATE CAPITOL TALLAHASSEE 32301
GEORGIA	JOHNNIE L. CALDWELL INSURANCE COMMISSIONER	238 STATE CAPITOL ATLANTA 30334
HAWAII	SUSAN PARK INSURANCE COMMISSIONER	P. O. BOX 3416 HONOLULU 96811

STATE	NAME AND TITLE	ADDRESS
IDAHO	TRENT M. WOODS DIRECTOR OF INSURANCE	700 WEST STATE ST. BOISE 83720
ILLINOIS	JAMES W. SCHACHT DIRECTOR OF INSURANCE	320 W. WASHINGTON ST. SPRINGFIELD 62767
INDIANA	DON H. MILLER COMMISSIONER OF INSURANCE	509 STATE OFFICE BLDG. INDIANAPOLIS 46204
IOWA	BRUCE W. FOUNDREE COMMISSIONER OF INSURANCE	STATE OFFICE BLDG. SUITE G23 DES MOINES 50319
KANSAS	FLETCHER BELL COMMISSIONER OF INSURANCE	420 S.W. 9TH STREET TOPEKA 66612
KENTUCKY	DANIEL D. BRISCOE INSURANCE COMMISSIONER	151 ELKHORN ST. FRANKFORT 40601
LOUISIANA	SHERMAN BERNARD COMMISSIONER OF INSURANCE	950 N. 5TH STREET BATON ROUGE, 70801
MAINE	THEODORE T. BRIGGS SUPERINTENDENT OF INSURANCE	STATE OFFICE BLDG. AUGUSTA 04333
MARYLAND	EDWARD J. MUHL INSURANCE COMMISSIONER	501 ST. PAUL PLACE BALTIMORE 21202
MASSACHUSETTS	MICHAEL J. SABBAGH COMMISSIONER OF INSURANCE	100 CAMBRIDGE STREET BOSTON 02202
MICHIGAN	NANCY A. BAERWALDT INSURANCE COMMISSIONER	P. O. BOX 30220 LANSING 48909
MINNESOTA	THOMAS L. O'MALLEY COMMISSIONER OF INSURANCE	500 METRO SQUARE BLVD. ST. PAUL 55101
MISSISSIPPI	GEORGE DALE COMMISSIONER OF INSURANCE	P. O. BOX 79 JACKSON 39205
MISSOURI	C. DONALD AINSWORTH DIRECTOR OF INSURANCE	P. O. BOX 690 JEFFERSON CITY 65102

STATE	NAME AND TITLE	ADDRESS
MONTANA	ELMER V. OMHOLT COMMISSIONER OF INSURANCE	P. O. BOX 4009 HELENA 56901
NEBRASKA	WALTER D. WEAVER DIRECTOR OF INSURANCE	P. O. BOX 94699 LINCOLN 68509
NEVADA	PATSY REDMOND COMMISSIONER OF INSURANCE	201 SOUTH FALL STREET CARSON CITY 89710
NEW HAMPSHIRE	FRANK E. WHALAND INSURANCE COMMISSIONER	P. O. BOX 2005 CONCORD 03301
NEW JERSEY	JOSEPH F. MURPHY COMMISSIONER OF INSURANCE	201 E. STATE STREET TRENTON 08625
NEW MEXICO	VINCENTE B. JASSO SUPERINTENDENT OF INSURANCE	P. O. DRAWER 1269 SANTA FE 87501
NEW YORK	ALBERT B. LEWIS SUPERINTENDENT OF INSURANCE	TWO WORLD TRADE CENTER NEW YORK 10047
N. CAROLINA	JOHN R. INGRAM COMMISSIONER OF INSURANCE	P. O. BOX 26387 RALEIGH 27611
N. DAKOTA	J. O. WIGEN COMMISSIONER OF INSURANCE	CAPITOL BLDG. 5TH FLOOR
OHIO	ROBERT L. RATCHFORD, JR. DIRECTOR OF INSURANCE	2100 STELLA COURT COLUMBUS 43215
OKLAHOMA	GERALD GRIMES INSURANCE COMMISSIONER	408 WILL RODGERS MEMORIAL BUILDING OKLAHOMA CITY 73105
OREGON	JOSEPHINE M. DRISCOLL INSURANCE COMMISSIONER	158 12TH STREET, N.E. SALEM 97310
PENNSYLVANIA	MICHAEL L. BROWNE INSURANCE COMMISSIONER	STRAWBERRY SQUARE HARRISBURG 17120
RHODE ISLAND	THOMAS J. CALDARONE, JR. INSURANCE COMMISSIONER	100 NORTH MAIN ST. PROVIDENCE 02903

STATE	NAME AND TITLE	ADDRESS
S. CAROLINA	ROGERS T. SMITH INSURANCE COMMISSIONER	P. O. BOX 4067 COLUMBIA 29204
S. DAKOTA	HENRY J. LUSSEM, JR. DIRECTOR OF INSURANCE	INSURANCE BUILDING PIERRE 57501
TENNESSEE	JOHN C. NEFF COMMISSIONER OF INSURANCE	114 STATE OFFICE ST. NASHVILLE 37219
TEXAS	E. J. VOORHIS COMMISSIONER OF INSURANCE	1100 SAN JACINTO BLVD. AUSTIN 78786
UTAH	ROGER C. DAY COMMISSIONER OF INSURANCE	326 SOUTH 5TH EAST SALT LAKE CITY 84102
VERMONT	GEORGE A. CHAFFEE COMMISSIONER OF INSURANCE	STATE OFFICE BUILDING MONTPELIER 05602
VIRGINIA	JAMES M. THOMSON COMMISSIONER OF INSURANCE	P. O. BOX 1157 RICHMOND 23209
WASHINGTON	RICHARD C. MARQUARDT INSURANCE COMMISSIONER	INSURANCE BLDG. ROOM AQ 21 OLYMPIA 98504
W. VIRGINIA	RICHARD G. SHAW INSURANCE COMMISSIONER	2100 WASHINGTON ST., E. CHARLESTON 25305
WISCONSIN	ANN J. HANEY COMMISSIONER OF INSURANCE	123 W. WASHINGTON AVE. MADISON 53207
WYOMING	JOHN T. LANGDON INSURANCE COMMISSIONER	2424 PIONEER AVE. CHEYENNE 82002

BAIL BOND FEES

STATE	AMOUNT
Alabama	10%
Alaska	10% AND $10 FOR BONDS UNDER $500
Arizona	10% AND $10 FOR BONDS UNDER $500
Arkansas	10% ($10 MINIMUM)
California	10% AND $10 FOR BONDS UNDER $500
Colorado	10%
Connecticut	10% TO $5000; 7% OVER $5000 ($20 MINIMUM)
Delaware	10% ($25 MINIMUM)
Florida	10% ($10 MINIMUM); 15% FEDERAL BONDS
Georgia	10% TO $500; 5% OVER $500
Hawaii	10%
Idaho	10% ($25 MINIMUM)
Illinois	10%
Indiana	10%
Iowa	10% ($25 MINIMUM)
Kansas	10% ($20 MINIMUM)
Kentucky	10% AND EXPENSES
Louisiana	10% ($30 MINIMUM)

BAIL BOND FEES

STATE	AMOUNT
Maryland	7% CITY BONDS; 10% COUNTY BONDS; 15% FEDERAL BONDS; ($25 MINIMUM)
Massachusetts	10%
Michigan	10%
Minnesota	10%
Mississippi	10%; 15% FEDERAL BONDS; TRAVEL EXPENSES OF $.15 PER MILE
Missouri	10% COUNTY BONDS; 20% CITY BONDS
Montana	10% AND $10 UNDER $500
Nebraska	10% AND $20 SERVICE CHARGE
Nevada	10% AND $10 UNDER $500
New Hampshire	10%
New Jersey	10% TO $2500; 6% OVER $2500
New Mexico	10% AND $10 UNDER $500
New York	5% FIRST $1000; 4% TO $2000; 3% OVER $2000
North Carolina	15%
North Dakota	10% AND TRAVEL EXPENSES ($35 MINIMUM)
Oklahoma	10% AND TRAVEL EXPENSES
Ohio	10% AND TRAVEL EXPENSES
Oregon	10% AND $15 UNDER $1000

BAIL BOND FEES

STATE	AMOUNT
Pennsylvania	10% TO $500; 7% OVER $500
Rhode Island	10%
South Carolina	10% AND TRAVEL EXPENSES
South Dakota	10% AND $.25 PER MILE
Tennessee	10%
Texas	15%
Utah	10% AND EXPENSES ($10 MINIMUM)
Vermont	10% $25 MINIMUM
Virginia	10% STATE; 10% FEDERAL ($20 MINIMUM
Washington	10% AND $15 UNDER $500
West Virginia	10% ($25 MINIMUM)
Wisconsin	10%
Wyoming	10% AND EXPENSES ($20 MINIMUM)

SURETY INSURANCE COMPANIES

The surety insurance companies listed below are agencies that write bail bonds. You should contact them to find out their requirements for someone who wants to write bonds for their insurance company. When calling these companies ask for the "bail bond" division. Also check the yellow pages in the business telephone directory under "Bonds - Surety & Fidelity".

AMERICAN BANKERS INSURANCE COMPANY
11222 Quail Roost Drive
Miami, FL 33157
(305) 253-2244

AMWEST SURETY INSURANCE COMPANY
P.O. Box 4500
Woodland Hills, California 91365-4500
Attention: Court Division
(818) 704-1111

BAIL U.S.A.
P.O. Box 806
Greenville, PA 16125
(412) 588-4377

CALIFORNIA RESIDENTS ONLY:

For information regarding Pre-Licensing Education for Bail Bonds contact the following agency:

CALIFORNIA BAIL AGENTS ASSOCIATION
1127 11TH St.
Sacramento, CA 95814
(916) 446-3038

POLICE CODES: 10 CODES

POLICE CODES

Police communications will always be the backbone of police tactics and never more so than today when radio and television are being used so effectively in crime prevention and detection. To facilitate more rapid communication codes have been devised where one or two words can tell the whole story. It is worth noting that the codes used principally for saving air time and not for security reasons. Two basic codes are in use with many variations. They are usually called the Nine Code and the Ten Code. In recent years the latter code has been gaining favor. The Association of Police Communications Officers has for some time been urging the standardization of such codes with the adoption of the Ten Code.

Ten Code

CODE 1 —Your Convenience
CODE 2 —Urgent—No red light and siren
CODE 3 —Emergency—Use red light and siren
CODE 4 —No further assistance needed
CODE 5 —Stakeout
CODE 6M—Misdemeanor Want
CODE 6F—Felony Want
CODE 6AD—Felony Want—Armed and dangerous
CODE 7 —Mealtime
CODE 8 —Box alarm
CODE 10 —Bomb threat
CODE 20 —Assist officer—urgent
CODE 30 —Officer needs help Emergency
CODE 33 —Emergency in progress—Do not transmit
187 Murder
207 Kidnapping
211 Robbery
245 ADW
288 L. & L. conduct
261 Rape
311 Indecent exposure
415 Disturbance
415F Family disturbance
460 Burglary
480 Felony hit and run
481 Misd. hit and run
487 Grand Theft
488 Petty Theft
502 Drunk Driver
503 Stolen vehicle
505 Reckless driving
647 Vagrant
510 Vehicle speeding
647A Child molest
1000 Plane crash
3000 Road Blockade
5050 Insane person
904 Fire
950 Burning permit fire
952 Report on conditions
953 Smoke investigation
953A Gas investigation
955 Fire under control
10-1 Receiving poor
10-2 Receiving OK
10-4 Message received—OK
10-5 Relay to
10-7 Out of service at:
10-7B Out of service, personal
10-70D Off duty
10-8 In service
10-8X In serv. w/female. Mileage:
10-9 Repeat
10-10 Out of service at home
10-12 Visitors or officials present
10-13 Weather and road conditions
10-14 Escort
10-14F Funeral detail
10-15 Have prisoner in custody
10-16 Pickup
10-19 Return to/enroute station
10-20 Location
10-21 Phone your office, or:
10-21A Phone home my eta is:
10-21B Phone your home
10-21R Phone radio
10-22 Cancel
10-23 Standby
10-25 Do you have contact with:
10-28 Registration
10-29 Check for wanted
10-32 Drowning
10-33 Alarm sounding
10-34 Open door
10-35 Open window
10-39 Status of:
10-40 Is .... available for phone call
10-45 Ambulance, injured
10-46 Ambulance, sick
10-49 Proceed to:
10-50 Obtain a report
10-51 Drunk
10-52 Resuscitator
10-53 Man down
10-54 Possible dead body
10-55 Coroner's case
10-56 Suicide
10-56A Attempted suicide
10-57 Firearms discharged
10-58 Garbage complaint
10-59 Malicious mischief
10-62 Meet the citizen
10-65 Missing person
10-66 Suspicious person
10-67 Person calling for help
10-70 Prowler
10-71 Shooting
10-72 Knifing
10-73 How do you receive
10-80 Explosion
10-86 Any traffic for:
10-87 Meet officer
10-91 Stray animal
10-91A Vicious animal
10-91B Noisy animal
10-91C Injured animal
10-91D Dead animal
10-91E Animal bite
10-91F Sick animal
10-91H Stray horses
10-97 Arrived at the scene
10-98 Finished with last assignment
11-24 Abandoned vehicle
11-26 Abondoned bicycle
11-54 Suspicious vehicle
11-79 Accident—ambulance enroute
11-80 Accident—Major injury
11-81 Accident—Minor injury
11-82 Accident—property damage
11-83 Accident—no detail
11-84 Traffic control
11-96 Leaving the vehicle to investigate an auto. If not heard from within 10 min. dispatch cover. (Give license and location)

POLICE CODES: 900 CODE

900 Code

Use suffix X whenever woman involved.

187	Murder
207	Kidnapping
211	Robbery
245	Assault with deadly weapon
288	Lewd and lascivious conduct
311	Indecent exposure of person
311A	Indecent exposure of pictures, etc.
415	Disturbing the peace
415A	In automobile
415B	Boys
415C	Investigate trouble
415D	Drunkenness involved
415E	Music or party involved
415F	Family row
415G	Gang
460	Burglary
480	Felony hit and run
481	Misdemeanor hit and run
484	Theft—petty
484A	Theft—grand
501	Felony—drunk driving
502	Misdemeanor—drunk driving
503	Auto theft
505	Reckless driving
1000	Plane crash
2000	Prison or jail break (many)
2000A	Escaped prisoner
3000	Saboteurs
4000	Convoy—wide load A—Army C—Civilian E—Evacuation N—Navy R—Red Cross W—A.W.V.S.
5050	Insane case
900	Emergency info.—stand by without using two-way
901	Vehicle accident property
901A	Vehicle accident injury
901B	Ascertain if ambulance needed
901D	Vehicle accident drunk
902	Check in vicinity
903	Traffic congestion
905	Abandoned automobile
905B	Abandoned bicycle
906	Person breaking in
907	Peeping tom
908	Out of service
908A	Meals
908A	Personal
908C	At home
908D	Off duty
909	In service
909A	In service from meals
909B	On duty
910	Prowler outside
910A	Prowler inside
911	Person shot
911A	Person stabbed
911B	Person slugged
912	Suspicious man
912X	Suspicious woman
913	Suicide (man)
913A	Suicide attempt
913X	Suicide (woman)
914	Phone your station
915	Phone radio station
916	Domestic trouble—weapons involved
917	Serious disturbance—possible felony
918	Person screaming for help
918X	Woman screaming
919	Drunk rolling in progress
920	Gasoline thefts
921	Car prowler or clouter
922	Drunk—on street
922A	Drunk in or about car
922B	Drunk in building
922C	Drunk in park or public place
923	Begging on street
923A	Begging in park or public
923A	Beggar ringing door bells
923C	Begging in stores
923D	Begging in office buildings
924	Go to your station
924A	Go to your station—urgent
925	Go to your radio station
925A	Go to your radio station urgent
925B	Close signal box
926	Give your location
926A	Repeat your message
927	Bonfire—investigate
928	Explosion
929	Fire
930	Signals weak—change location
931	Accident—auto not involved
932	Drowning
933	Burglar or bank alarm sounding
934	Major emergency or disaster go to assigned or predetermined post at once
935	License information
936	File check on vehicle
936A	File check on person
936B	File check on description
936C	File check on address
936D	File check on phone number
938	Cancel your last assignment
940	Meet the officer
940A	Officer needs assistance
941	Citizen holding prisoner
942	Pick up prisoner
942A	Pick up papers
942B	Pick up officer
942D	Pick up a teletype
942M	Pick up the matron
943	Fight (battery) no weapons
944	Civil disturbance (riots)
945	Ambulance follow-up needed
946	Tow car needed
947	Patrol wagon needed
949	Investigate suspicious occupants in auto
950	Get report from man
950X	Get report from woman
953A	Sick man
954	Road blockade
955	Animals straying
955A	Vicious animal
955B	Noisy animal
955C	Injured animal
955E	Dog bite
956	Peddling without license
957	Firearms unlawful discharge
958	Garbage disposal—improper
959	Malicious mischief
960	Trepassing
960A	Vehicle involved
960B	Animal involved
961	Window breaker
962	Meet a citizen
963	Ball playing in street
964	Reserved
965	Lost child
970	Improperly parked auto
970A	On sidewalk
970B	Front of driveway or garage
970C	In front of restricted zone
994	Drills or tests or plans
999	Radio silence

APPLICATION FOR BAIL LICENSE

STATE OF CALIFORNIA

JOHN GARAMENDI, *Insurance Commissioner*

DEPARTMENT OF INSURANCE
700 L STREET
SACRAMENTO, CA 95814

Information (916) 322-3555

To: BAIL LICENSE APPLICANTS

California Code of Regulations, Section 2077.1 requires this department to issue an identification card to all bail licensees.

To issue this identification card we require that you submit two recently taken, 1 1/4" X 1 1/4" full face photographs with your application for bail license.

Place the photographs inside an envelope, seal and staple the envelope to the inside of your application.

Failure to submit your photographs at the time of filing the application may result in a delay in the issuance of your license.

Sidney J. Gauthreaux

Chief, License Bureau

TE OF CALIFORNIA

DEPARTMENT OF INSURANCE
P.O. BOX 398
SAN FRANCISCO, CA 94101

APPLICATION FOR BAIL LICENSE

READ THE INSTRUCTIONS ON PAGE 4 BEFORE COMPLETING THIS APPLICATION

FOR DEPARTMENT USE ONLY

FILE NUMBER ALPHA

1

2 WK STA ENTITY

3 PERM ISSUED PRINT

PERM MAILED

4 DBA AKA

5 THRU DATE

6 RESTR

LICENSE TYPE (Check the type(s) for which you are applying.):

☐ BAIL PERMITTEE ☐ BAIL AGENT ☐ BAIL SOLICITOR

APPLICANT NAME:

Last ______

First Middle

IDENTIFICATION INFORMATION:

▶ ATTACH A RECENT 1¼x1¼ PHOTOGRAPH:

Social Security Number ___ ___ ___ - ___ ___ - ___ ___ ___ ___

Sex: ___ Male ___ Female Birth Date ___ - ___ - ___

Birthplace ______

Height ___ Weight ___ Hair Color ___ Eye Color ___

BUSINESS ADDRESS: (P.O. Box not acceptable)

Street ______ Apt/Suite # ______

City State Zip

MAILING ADDRESS:

PO Box/Street ______ Apt/Suite # ______

City State Zip

RESIDENCE ADDRESS FOR LAST TWO YEARS: (P.O. Box not acceptable)

A **CURRENT** RESIDENCE:

Street ______ Apt/Suite # ______

City ______ State ______ Zip ______

B **PRIOR** RESIDENCE:

Date Resided From	To	Street	Apt/Suite #	City	State

EXAMINATION INFORMATION:

Desired Location ______ (LA) Los Angeles, (SD) San Diego, (SF) San Francisco, (SA) Sacramento, (FR) Fresno

Desired Date ______ a.m. ______ p.m. ______ If we are unable to honor this date, the next available date will be scheduled.

DO YOU INTEND TO USE A FICTITIOUS (DBA) NAME TO CONDUCT YOUR BAIL BUSINESS .... ☐ YES ☐ NO

If **YES**, list such name: (This name must be approved by the Department prior to use).

ARE YOU NOW USING OR HAVE YOU EVER USED ANY NAME OTHER THAN LISTED IN (2), or (8)? .... ☐ YES ☐ NO

If **YES**, list names, dates and reason used.

______

______

10	DO YOU NOW HOLD, OR HAVE YOU EVER HELD, ANY LICENSE/PERMIT UNDER WHICH YOU ENGAGED IN ANY OCCUPATION? .... ☐ YES ☐ N If YES, list such license/permit:

Type of License and License Number	State or Province	Resident or Nonresident	Date License held From	To	Is Licens In Force

11

A. LIST YOUR OCCUPATION/EMPLOYMENT FOR THE PAST *FIVE* YEARS TO *CURRENT* DATE — Include unemployment and school.

From (Mo. & Yr.)	To (Mo. & Yr.)	Employer Name	Address	Duties Performed	Reason For Leaving

B. IF CURRENTLY EMPLOYED, WILL YOU CONTINUE THIS OCCUPATION AFTER RECEIVING THE LICENSE FOR WHICH THIS APPLICATION IS BEING MADE? .... ☐ YES ☐ N

12

BAIL AGENT APPLICANTS ONLY:

A. WILL UNDERTAKING OF BAIL BE SUPPLIED TO YOU THROUGH A GENERAL AGENT OR OTHER INTERMEDIARY? .... ☐ YES ☐ N

If you answer **YES**, give the name of such person ____________

B. WILL YOU OR ANYONE ELSE MAKE A DEPOSIT OF MONEY OR THING OF VALUE TO ESTABLISH AN INITIAL RESERVE ACCOUNT FOR YOU? .... ☐ YES ☐ N

If you answer **YES**, complete the following:

Describe the type of deposit (i.e., cash, securities, real property, etc.) ____________

What is the value thereof? ____________

With whom will such deposit be made? ____________

By whom will such deposit be made? ____________

13

BAIL AGENT AND/OR PERMITTEE APPLICANTS ONLY:

WILL ANY PERSON, OTHER THAN YOURSELF, RECEIVE ANY INCOME OR REMUNERATION FROM YOUR BAIL BUSINESS? .... ☐ YES ☐ N

(Exclude your employees, your employing bail agent/permittee, your general agent and the appointing surety.)

If you answer **YES**, give the following information for each person who will receive such income or remuneration:

NAME LAST	FIRST	MIDDLE	RESIDENCE ADDRESS	INTEREST OR AFFILIATION

14

BAIL PERMITTEE APPLICANTS ONLY:

Attach a detailed current financial statement listing the dollar amount of each of your **assets, liabilities,** and **net worth,** (i.e., personal property, real estate, savings, household furnishings, etc.)

15 **IF APPLICANT OR APPLICANT'S EMPLOYER IS A PARTNERSHIP, COMPLETE THE FOLLOWING:** (Attach a separate sheet if more space is needed.)

A. PARTNERSHIP NAME: ______________________

B.

PARTNERS NAMES Last / First / Middle	BAIL LICENSE NUMBER	If **not** licensed, list their functions/responsibility within the partnership

16 **IF YOU ANSWER *YES* TO ANY OF THE FOLLOWING QUESTIONS A, B. OR C, ATTACH A SUPPLEMENTARY STATEMENT GIVING COMPLETE DETAILS:**

A. Are you now or have you ever been connected with a law enforcement agency? . . . . ☐ YES ☐ NO

B. Have you ever been named as a defendant in a civil suit? . . . . ☐ YES ☐ NO

C. Have you ever filed bankruptcy? . . . . ☐ YES ☐ NO

▶ **IMPORTANT NOTICE:** If you answer yes to (17), or (18), attach a detailed statement of the events which led to the charges (dates and places). If the matter was heard in court, attach copies, certified by the court, of the **Criminal** Complaint and the Sentencing Minute Order showing the final judgment.

17 **HAVE YOU *EVER* HAD ANY PROFESSIONAL, VOCATIONAL OR BUSINESS LICENSE DENIED, SUSPENDED, REVOKED OR RESTRICTED OR A FINE IMPOSED BY ANY PUBLIC AUTHORITY, OR WITHDRAWN ANY APPLICATION FOR OR SURRENDERED ANY SUCH LICENSE TO AVOID DISCIPLINARY ACTION?** . . . . ☐ YES ☐ NO

18 **HAVE YOU *EVER* BEEN CONVICTED OF A CRIME?** . . . . ☐ YES ☐ NO

"Crime" includes a felony or misdemeanor and military offenses. "Convicted" includes, but is not limited to, having been found guilty by verdict of a judge or jury, having entered a plea of nolo contendere, having had any charge dismissed or plea withdrawn pursuant to Penal Code Section 1203.4, or having been given probation, a suspended sentence or a fine. You may exclude traffic citations and juvenile offenses.

19 **APPLICANT'S STATEMENT AND CERTIFICATION:**

I DECLARE THAT I HAVE READ SECTIONS 2053 THROUGH 2104 OF TITLE 10 OF THE CALIFORNIA CODE OF REGULATIONS.

I REPRESENT THAT THE HOLDING OF THE LICENSE HEREBY APPLIED FOR IS NOT INCOMPATIBLE WITH THE LAW, RULES OR REGULATIONS OF ANY FEDERAL, STATE, COUNTY, OR MUNICIPAL GOVERNMENT BY WHICH I AM CURRENTLY EMPLOYED (IF ANY) OR BY WHICH MY EMPLOYER OR I AM LICENSED (IF ANY).

I CERTIFY UNDER PENALTY OF PERJURY THAT I HAVE READ THE FOREGOING APPLICATION AND KNOW THE CONTENTS THEREOF AND THAT EACH STATEMENT THEREIN MADE IS FULL, TRUE AND CORRECT, AND I AGREE TO NOTIFY THE INSURANCE COMMISSIONER OF ANY CHANGE IN THE MATTERS SET FORTH IN THIS APPLICATION. I UNDERSTAND THAT PURSUANT TO SECTIONS 1668 (h) AND 1738 OF THE INSURANCE CODE ANY FALSE STATEMENT MAY SUBJECT BY APPLICATION TO DENIAL AND MAY SUBJECT MY LICENSE(S) TO SUSPENSION OR REVOCATION. FURTHER, PURSUANT TO INSURANCE CODE SECTIONS 1703 AND 1733, I AUTHORIZE DISCLOSURE TO THE INSURANCE COMMISSIONER OF ALL FINANCIAL INSTITUTION RECORDS OF ANY FIDUCIARY ACCOUNTS FOR THE DURATION OF THIS LICENSE.

▶ APPLICANT'S SIGNATURE ______________ ▶ CITY ________ ▶ DATE ________

▶ BUSINESS PHONE # (   ) ______________ ▶ RESIDENCE PHONE # (   ) ______________

NOTICE: INFORMATION COLLECTION AND ACCESS

Section 1798.17 of the California Civil Code requires the following information to be provided when collecting information from individuals.

AGENCY: Department of Insurance

TITLE OF OFFICIAL RESPONSIBLE FOR INFORMATION MAINTENANCE: Chief, License Bureau

ADDRESS: 700 L Street, Sacramento, CA 95814

TELEPHONE NUMBER: (916) 322-3555

AUTHORITY WHICH AUTHORIZES THE MAINTENANCE OF THE INFORMATION: California Insurance Code, Chapter 5, 6, 7, 8-Part 2, Division 1.

THE PRINCIPAL PURPOSE(S) FOR WHICH THE INFORMATION IS TO BE USED: Evaluation of license application.

EACH INDIVIDUAL HAS THE RIGHT TO REVIEW FILES MAINTAINED ON THEM BY THE AGENCY, UNLESS THE INFORMATION IS CLASSIFIED AS CONFIDENTIAL UNDER SECTION 1798.3(a) OF THE CIVIL CODE.

FILING INSTRUCTIONS

1. All entries, except signatures, must be typed.
2. Application for license must be filed with the Department promptly after being executed, and be completed in full, signed, dated and accompanied by all required fees and supplementary documents. Deficient filings will require amending and result in processing delays.
3. All applicants are required to be fully knowledgeable in the rules and regulations governing bail bond transactions covered in Sections 2053 through 2104 of the extracts of the California Code of Regulations.
4. Bond coverage is required for all bail licenses.
5. **Forms Filing List:** Each bail agent or permittee applying for license must provide a copy of the forms or documents which the licensee intends to use regularly or frequently in connection with his/her bail transactions [California Administrative Code, Section 2095 (k)]. As each surety has previously filed such forms, the bail agent applicant's compliance with Section 2095(k) can be accomplished by filing a forms list as provided by the surety. This signed list should accompany the application when it is filed with the Department.

   Note: Bail solicitors are exempt from this requirement as they will be utilizing their employer's forms in their transactions of bail.
6. A bail agent's and a permittee's license may be applied for at the same time by checking both appropriate boxes of section '1' of the application, in which case, only a permittee's bond is required. Also, if a currently licensed bail permittee is now applying for an agent's license, the permittee's bond on file will cover both licenses.
7. An Action Notice of Appointment (Form 437-23) from a surety company is required for a bail agent applicant. A separate filing fee is required for each subsequent appointment submitted with the application.
8. An Action Notice Statement (Form 438) from a bail agent or permittee is required for a bail solicitor applicant. If a bail solicitor applicant is to work for two or more bail licensees who are members of a partnership, a separate Action Notice Statement from each employer and an additional **filing** fee for each is required.
9. An Action Notice Statement (Form 438) from a Bail Agent or Bail Permittee is required when employing or terminating the employment of another licensed Bail Agent or Permittee.
10. All fictitious names must be approved by this department prior to use. Refer to California Code of Regulations 2066.4 for fictitious name filing requirements. If applying for a bail permittee's license, also refer to Sections 2094 and 2094.5
11. A written examination administered by the department is required if examination qualifications have not already been met. Examinations are administered daily Monday through Friday at 8:30 a.m. and 1:00 p.m. in Los Angeles, San Francisco, San Diego and Sacramento, and once monthly in Fresno, usually the third Saturday of the month.

    EXAMINATION INFORMATION: The qualifying examination consists of 50 questions based on:

    A) California Insurance Code Sections 35, 1733 and 1800 to 1822.
    B) California Code of Regulations, Title 10, Sections 2053 through 2103.
    C) California Penal Code, Sections 1268 through 1319.6.

    The Department of Insurance does not recommend any specific school, course or method of training to prepare for the bail examination.
12. Fingerprint impressions are required for all unlicensed applicants.
13. An applicant for license may not solicit, negotiate or transact bail until authorized to do so under an appropriate license issued by the Department. After all filing requirements are submitted, the applicant will be notified if a personal interview by the department is required.
14. Mail application filings with fees to: DEPARTMENT OF INSURANCE
P.O. BOX 398
SAN FRANCISCO, CA 94101

ALL FEES ARE FILING FEES AND ARE NOT REFUNDABLE OR TRANSFERABLE, WHETHER OR NOT THE APPLICATION IS ACTED UPON OR THE EXAMINATION TAKEN.

ABOUT THE AUTHOR

Richard Wills began his career in the bail bond business back in 1980. Working as a bondsman for several bonding companies in Los Angeles, he was exposed to the secret world of the bail bondsman. A unique researcher of business opportunities, Mr. Wills is considered an authority in his field.

Besides his contributions to national magazines, his marketing and consulting strategies have helped hundreds of individuals get on the right track in the bail bond business. He mixes his experience and knowledge as a research expert with assisting others in operating a successful bail bond business.

He is an author, screenwriter and publisher of several non-fiction works. In addition to "The Professional Bondsman — How To Start And Operate Your Own Bail Bond Agency (2nd Edition), his previous best seller"900 Gold™- Marketing Secrets For Success In The 900 Business" is now in it's second printing.

A native of Louisiana, Mr. Wills now lives in Southern California. If you wish to contact Mr. Wills for consultation or just to say hello, write: R. W. Associates, 4230 Del Rey Ave. Dept. 26, Marina Del Rey, California 90292.

To order additional copies of **The Professional Bondsman,** complete the information below.

Ship to: (please print)

Name ____

Address ____

City, ______________________________ State, ________ Zip _______________

Day Phone ____

______ copies of The Professional Bondsman @ $21.95 each $ ________

Postage and Handling @ $4.50 per book $ ________

California residents add 7.75% tax $ ________

Total amount enclosed $ ________

Make checks / money order payable to: **The Dragon Press**
4230 Del Rey Ave.

Marina Del Rey, CA 90292

FOR CREDIT CARD ORDERS ❑ VISA ❑ MASTERCARD:

Expiration Date ___________

Signature ____
Cardholder Signature Required To Process